FTCE

Florida Teacher Certification Exams

K-6 Subject Area Exam

English

Social Science

Science

Math

Kathleen Jasper, Ed.S
Edge Academic Solutions
Estero, Florida

Annmarie Ferry
Edge Academic Solutions
Estero, Florida

Jeremy Jasper, M.A.
Edge Academics Solutions
Estero, Florida

Edge Academic Solutions
10600 Chevrolet Way #223
Estero, FL 33928

FTCE - Elementary ED K-6 Subject Area Exam
1st Edition

Printed in the United States of America
ISBN-13: 978-1537257358 (CreateSpace-Assigned)
ISBN-10: 1537257358

The competencies in this book were designed and implemented by the Florida Department of
Education. Visit www.fl.nesinc.com for more information.

LIMIT OF LIABILITY/DISCLAIMER OF WARRANTY: Publication of this work is for the purpose
of test preparation and related use and subject set for herein. While every effort has been made
to achieve a work of high quality, the authors of this work do not assume any liability in
connection with this information.

Cover Image: © Amazon

FTCE - Elementary ED K-6 Subject Area Exam

Preparation Guide

III. Science   97

IV. Mathematics   145

I. English Language Arts

This chapter provides an overview of the competencies for the Language Arts and Reading section of Elementary ED (K-6) Subject Area Exam. This section has explanations regarding all the competencies tested on the exam as well as in-depth analysis of the types of questions students will encounter when taking this test.

The competencies addressed in this chapter are from the Florida Teacher Certification Examination Test Information Guide.

You can access that using this link:
http://www.fl.nesinc.com/PDFs/ElemEd_K-6_TIG_4thEd_DOE040115.pdf

Competency 1: Knowledge of the Reading Process

1. Identify the content of emergent literacy (e.g., oral language development, phonological awareness, alphabet knowledge, decoding, concepts of print, motivation, text structures, written language development).
2. Identify the processes, skills, and stages of word recognition that lead to effective decoding (e.g., pre-alphabetic, partial-alphabetic, full-alphabetic, graphophonemic, morphemic).
3. Select and apply instructional methods for the development of decoding skills (e.g., continuous blending, chunking).
4. Distinguish among the components of reading fluency (e.g., accuracy, automaticity, rate, prosody).
5. Choose and apply instructional methods for developing reading fluency (e.g., practice with high-frequency words, readers theatre, repeated readings).
6. Identify and differentiate instructional methods and strategies for increasing vocabulary acquisition across the content areas (e.g., word analysis, author's word choice, context clues, multiple exposures).
7. Identify and evaluate instructional methods and strategies for facilitating students' reading comprehension (e.g., summarizing, self-monitoring, questioning, use of graphic and semantic organizers, think alouds, recognizing story structure).
8. Identify essential comprehension skills (e.g., main idea, supporting details and facts, author's purpose, point of view, inference, conclusion).
9. Determine appropriate uses of multiple representations of information for a variety of purposes (e.g., charts, tables, graphs, pictures, print and nonprint media).
10. Determine and analyze strategies for developing critical-thinking skills such as analysis, synthesis, and evaluation (e.g., making connections and predictions, questioning, summarizing, question generating).
11. Evaluate and select appropriate instructional strategies for teaching a variety of informational and literary text.

Emergent Readers

Readers at this stage are learning to read and understand words by decoding the reading process as they engage with the text. Emergent literacy involves the skills, knowledge, and attitudes that are developmental precursors to conventional forms of reading and writing (Whitehurst & Lonigan, 1998). Emergent literacy skills begin developing in early infancy and early childhood through participation with adults in meaningful activities involving speaking and print.

Word recognition can be done in the following stages: pre-alphabetic, partial-alphabetic, full-alphabetic, consolidated-alphabetic (Ehri, 1999).

- **Pre-alphabetic phase**: students read words by memorizing visual features or guessing words from context.
- **Partial-alphabetic phase**: students recognize some letters and can use them to remember words by sight.
- **Full-alphabetic phase**: readers possess extensive working knowledge of the graphophonemic system, and they can use this knowledge to analyze fully the connections between graphemes and phonemes in words. They can decode unfamiliar words and store fully analyzed sight words in memory.
- **Consolidated-alphabetic phase**: students consolidate their knowledge of grapheme-phoneme blends into larger units that recur in different words.

Phonological awareness is the ability of the reader to recognize the sound of spoken language, including how sounds can be blended together, segmented (divided up), and manipulated (switched around).

Phonological awareness is the big umbrella the early reading skills **phonemic awareness** and **phonics** fall under.

> **Quick tip:**
> If students are **decoding** words, they are sounding them out as they read.

- **Phonemic awareness** - a sub-skill of phonological **awareness** in which students are able to hear, identify and manipulate **phonemes** (the smallest units of sound). For example, for a student to be able to separate the sounds in the word "cat" into three distinct **phonemes**, /k/, /æ/, and /t/, they must have **phonemic awareness**.
- **Phonics** - understanding correspondence between these sounds and the spelling patterns (graphemes) that represent them.
- **Graphophonemic (also referred to as phonics)** - the recognition of letters and the understanding of sound-symbol relationships and spelling patterns. **Graphophonemic** knowledge is often referred to as phonics.
- **Morphemic** - a form of spelling knowledge that focuses on the meaning of a word in its smallest form (morpheme) and how it changes when making compound words or using suffixes and prefixes.

Structural Analysis is the process of interpreting word parts that make up a word. This helps the reader determine the pronunciation and meaning of unknown words. This word identification technique is effective especially when used along with phonic analysis and context clues. Break the word down using its structure.

- **compound** words - two words put together (mailman, sidewalk)

- **prefixes** - additions to root words that help to form a new word with another meaning from that of the root word. Prefixes are at the beginning of a word.
  - Ex: prefixes that indicate "not": *un- (unknown), dis- (disregard), im- (impossible), in- (inaccurate), mis- (misunderstand),* and *ir- (irrational).*

> **Scenario:** Students are decoding words using the prefixes and suffixes to determine pronunciation and meaning. The students are engaging in a **structural analysis**. A teacher models how to break down compound words to understand the meaning of the words. the teacher and students are performing a **structural analysis**.

- **Suffixes** - additions to root words that form a new word with another meaning from that of the root word. Suffixes are at the end of a word. They change the part of speech (past tense, present tense), verb tense of a word. They also indicate whether the word is plural or singular.
  - Ex: -ed, -ing, and plural -s are all suffixes

Words can be broken down by:

- inflected forms (-s, -es, -ed, -ing, -ly)
- contractions
- possessives
- compound words
- syllables
- base words
- root words
- prefixes
- suffixes

- beginning consonants
- end consonants
- medial consonants
- consonant blends (*bl, gr, sp*)
- consonant digraphs (*sh, th, ch*)
- short vowels
- long vowels
- vowel pairs (*oo, ew, oi, oy*)

Blending - an important skill beginners use to mimic the process readers go through to sound out a word as in /p/-/a/-/t/ /pat/.
Onsets - beginning consonant and consonant cluster.
rimes - vowel and consonants that follow. Some common rimes are: *-ack, -an, -aw, -ick, -ing, -op, -unk, -ain, -ank, -ay, -ide, -ink, -or, -ock, -ight, -ame, -eat, -ine.*

Sight words are words that don't follow the rules. Students cannot use standard decoding and structure analysis on **sight words.** Students have to memorize sight words.

- want
- what
- why

- said
- see
- there

- by
- are

> **Scenario:** A teacher is helping her students memorize words like why, where and there. The students are using memorization for their **sight words** so they can read with fluency.

Early/Fluent Readers

Students at this stage have fluency and prosody. **Fluency** is reading without having to stop and decode (sound out) words. Fluency involves reading is reading a paragraph from start to finish with very few errors. **Prosody** is reading with expression using the words and punctuation correctly. Reading with prosody means you are conveying what's on the page, pausing at commas and periods, and using inflection based on punctuation.

Teachers perform **fluency checks** or a **fluency reads** to gauge students' reading progress. While the student reads, the teacher follows along. As the student reads, the teacher checks for **automaticity**, or how automatically the student is reading. Is the student decoding too often? Or, can the student automatically say words as she moves down the passage? The teacher also checks the student's **accuracy**, or correct pronunciation and reading of words. In addition, the teacher keeps track of the student's **rate,** or how many words the student reads per minute.

Teaching strategies to increase and monitor fluency:

- **Choral Reading** - reading aloud in unison with a whole class or group of students. Choral reading helps build students' fluency, self-confidence, and motivation.
- **Running Records** - following along as a student reads and marking when he or she makes a mistake or **miscues**.
- **Miscue Analysis** - looking over the running record and analyzing why the student miscued. Then the teacher can employ strategies to help the student with miscues

> **Scenario:** A teacher is following along as a student is reading. The teacher makes a mark whenever the student struggles or incorrectly says a word. After the student is done reading, both the teacher and student look over the miscues and discuss why the student miscued and how they can fix the problem. The teacher and student are engaging in a **fluency read, a running record, and a miscue analysis.**

Comprehension and Critical Thinking

Comprehension is the essence of reading. This is when students begin to form images in their minds as they read. They are able to predict what might happen next in a story because they understand what's happening in the story. Students who are in the comprehension stage of reading do not need to decode (sound out) words. They read **fluently** with **prosody, automaticity,** and **accuracy**.

Critical thinking is a high-level cognitive skill. This is when students can apply certain concepts to their reading. They may be able to come up with their own ending of the story or even an extra scene. This is when they are thinking deeply using evaluation and analysis in their reading.

Strategies for boosting **comprehension** and **critical thinking** are:

- **Predicting** - asking students what they think will happen next.
- **Questioning** - having students ask questions based on what they are reading.
- **Read aloud think aloud** - teacher or student reads and stops to think around about what the text means.
- **Summarizing** - asking students to summarize what they just read in their own words.

> **Scenario:**
> A teacher wants students to understand the book she is reading to the class. She stops to think aloud and talk out certain aspects of the story as she reads. She is using a **read aloud think aloud** technique to increase students' **meta cognition**, **critical thinking** and **comprehension**.

*All of these strategies can be employed before, during and after reading.

Know the three cuing systems:

1. **Syntactic:** The syntactic cuing system focuses on the structure of the sentence.

> **Scenario:**
> A student writes: ***I no go to park***. This is a syntactic issue. You can understand the meaning so this is not a semantic issue. The problem is in the structure of the sentence.

2. **Semantic:** The semantic cuing system focuses on the meaning a student derives from text.

3. **Graphophonemic:** The graphophonemic cuing system focuses on the relationship between sounds and symbols. For example: Letter/sound recognition.

Competency 2: Knowledge of literary analysis and genres

1. Differentiate among characteristics and elements of a variety of literary genres (e.g., realistic fiction, fantasy, poetry, informational texts).
2. Identify and analyze terminology and intentional use of literary devices (e.g., simile, metaphor, personification, onomatopoeia, hyperbole).
3. Evaluate and select appropriate multicultural texts based on purpose, relevance, cultural sensitivity, and developmental appropriateness.
4. Identify and evaluate appropriate techniques for varying student response to texts (e.g., think-pair-share, reading response journals, evidence-based discussion).

Literary Genres

Poems

Narrative poetry is a form of **poetry** that tells a story, often making use of the voices of a narrator and characters as well; the entire story is usually written in metered verse. The **poems** that make up this genre may be short or long, and the story it relates to may be complex.

Fixed Verse vs Free Verse
Fixed verse poetry has a set formula; free **verse** poetry has little or no pre-established guidelines.

Epic Poetry Originating in Greece, this long narrative focuses on the trials and tribulations of a hero or god-like character, who represents the cultural values of a race, nation, or religious group. The fate of the people is in the hands of the hero. Epic poetry typically takes place in a vast setting, and covers a wide geographic area. The protagonist in an epic poem possesses superhuman abilities and must prove himself or herself via feats of strength. Gods or supernatural beings frequently take part in the action to affect the outcome.

> **Quick Tip**:
> The purpose of poetry is to convey images. Not all poems rhyme. Not all poems are short or long. But **all** poems convey images.

A Haiku is a Japanese poem consisting of 3 lines and 17 syllables.

Quick Tip:
A teacher might use a Haiku poem to teach students syllabification.

Each line has a set number of syllables:
- Line 1 – 5 syllables
- Line 2 – 7 syllables
- Line 3 – 5 syllables

Example
(5) The sky is so blue.
(7) The sun is so warm up high.
(5) I love the summer.

A limerick is often a funny poem with a strong beat. Limericks are very light hearted poems and can sometimes be utter nonsense. They are great for kids to both read and write as they are short and funny.

The Structure of a Limerick Poem
- A limerick consists of five lines.
- The first line of a limerick poem usually begins with 'There was a....' and ends with a name, person or place.
- The last line of a limerick is normally a little farfetched or unusual.
- A limerick should have a rhyme scheme of aabba:

An example of a Limerick Poem by famous poet Edward Lear
'There was an old man with a beard
Who said, 'It is just as I feared,
Two owls and a hen
A lark and a wren
Have all built their nests in my beard!'

Sonnet
A sonnet is a poem of an expressive thought or idea made up of 14 lines, each 10 syllables long.

An example of a Sonnet Poem
a letter to my love
thanking god above
for the pen write
for my love tonight
who I hold so tight
as miss the smell
of her outer shell
always on my mind…

Literary Devices

Authors use **literary devices** to convey messages in a figurative manner. When employed properly, the different literary devices help readers to appreciate, interpret and analyze a literary work.

Types of literary devices		
Device	**Definition**	**Examples**
Simile	Using like or as.	She was **as thin as a rail.**
Metaphor	Applying word or phrase to an individual.	**He was a lion** filled with rage.
Personification	Attributing human characteristics to something not human.	**The cat judged me** from across the room.
Onomatopoeia	The formation of a word from a sound associated with it.	**Sizzle, Kurplunk, Pow, Bam**
Hyperbole	Exaggerated statements or claims not meant to be taken literally.	He must have **weighed 500 pounds!**

Multiculturalism

Prior to the 1960s, people who were not European or European American were virtually invisible in children's literature, or they were depicted in negative and/or stereotypical representations (Aoki, 1993; Nieto, 1997). It is important teachers represent all cultures when selecting books and posters for their classroom.

Ways in which teachers can be sure they are fostering multiculturalism in the classroom:

- Select literature with heroic characters that represent the culture of the classroom.
- Use picture books to convey multicultural messages.
- Encourage students to share stories of their culture with other students.
- Motivate all students to participate in celebrations, dances, and other activities that express multiculturalism.

Student Response to Text

Allowing students to respond and express themselves as they engage in text is a big part of the reading process. This can be done in a variety of engaging ways through written and oral activities.

Student Response to Text		
Activity	**Defintion**	**Example**
Jigsaw	A cooperative learning activity in which each student becomes an expert on a small piece of information that is part of a much larger piece.	Teachers arrange students in groups. Each group member is assigned a different piece of information. Group members then join with members of other groups assigned the same piece of information, and research and/or share ideas about the information. Eventually, students return to their original groups to try to "piece together" a clear picture of the topic at hand.
Think-Pair-Share	A cooperative learning activity in which students work together to solve a problem or answer a question about an assigned reading.	**Think** - Teachers begin by asking a specific question about the text. Students "think" about what they know or have learned about the topic. **Pair** - Each student should be paired with another student or a small group. **Share** - Students share their thinking with their partner. Teachers expand the "share" into a whole-class discussion.
Reading Response Journals	A writing activity where students use journals to react to what they read by expressing how they feel and asking questions about the text.	After reading a story book in class, the teacher asks students to use their reading response journals to respond to the story emotionally, make associations between ideas in the text and their own ideas, and questions they may have about the story.
Evidence-Based Discussion	Setting the expectation that students use evidence in the text to support claims they make during the discussion.	The class is discussing World War II. Students are split into groups and answer questions on the board. Students must identify where in the text is their answer or claim supported.
Literature Circles	A small-group, cooperative learning activity where students engage and discuss a piece of literature/text.	A teacher breaks students up into groups. Every student has a role. A teacher distributes an article from the news paper. Students read the discuss the article. Students engage using their role to understand the text.

Competency 3: Knowledge of language and the writing process.

1. Identify and evaluate the developmental stages of writing (e.g., drawing, dictating, writing).
2. Differentiate stages of the writing process (i.e., prewriting, drafting, revising, editing, publishing).
3. Distinguish among the modes of writing (e.g., narrative, informative/explanatory, argument).
4. Select the appropriate mode of writing for a variety of occasions, purposes, and audiences.
5. Identify and apply instructional methods for teaching writing conventions (e.g., spelling, punctuation, capitalization, syntax, word usage).
6. Apply instructional methods for teaching writer's craft across genres (e.g., precise language, figurative language, linking words, temporal words, dialogue, sentence variety).

Developmental Stages of Writing

Emergent Writing

Writing at this stage means that children begin to understand that writing is a form of communication and their marks on paper convey a message (Mayer, 2007).

> **Scenario**: A kindergarten student is using mock letters to represent words he understands but wants to convey on paper. This student is in the **emergent phase** of writing.

- **Preliterate (Drawing)** - The student uses drawing to stand for writing and believes that drawings/writing is communication of a purposeful message.
- **Preliterate (Scribbling)** - The student scribbles, but intends it as writing. The scribbling resembles writing. During this stage the student holds the pencil correctly.
- **Emergent** - The student uses random letters or drawings. Students at this stage also use letter sequences and may write long strings of numbers in random order.
- **Transitional** (could also be considered emergent) - Students at this stage use inventive spelling.

Fluent

Writing at this stage resembles adult writing. Grammar and spelling are mostly correct and one can read and understand what the writing says.

Pre- literate to Emergent	
Scribbling	Random marks or scribbles often occur on a page with drawings. Children may say, "This says Tommy!" (child's name). Toddlers use the terms drawing and writing to describe their marks; however, three- and four-year olds generally understand the difference between the two.
Emergent	
Mock Handwriting or Wavy Scribble	Children produce lines of wavy scribbles as they imitate adult cursive writing. Children will often pretend they are writing something they have seen their parents write such as a grocery list or letter.
Mock Letters	Children attempt to form alphabetic representations, which also often appear in their drawings. Writing in this stage is often vertical verses horizontal. Children make shapes that resemble conventional letters.
Conventional Letters	Children begin to write letters usually from their name or a family member's name. As children's mock letters become more and more conventional, real letters of the alphabet begin to appear. Children will often create "strings" of letters across a page and "read" them as real sentences or a series of sentences.
Invented Spelling (also known as Approximated Spelling)	Children write words using phonemic awareness. The words are not spelled correctly, but do resemble the sounds of the words. For example, inventive spelling of the word "was" may be "wuz" or the inventive spelling of the word "other" would be "uther."
Fluent	
Conventional Spellings	Children's approximated spellings gradually become more and more conventional. The child's own name is usually written first, followed by words such as mom, dad, and love. Initially children may incorrectly copy words. Eventually words will be written correctly. Adults can support the child's move to conventional spelling by being patient and by continuing to serve as a good writing model.

The Writing Process

Learning to write is similar to learning to read. There is a process young learners go through as they become writers of the English Language. Like reading the writing process has several stages:

Prewriting - brainstorming, considering purpose and goals for writing, using graphic organizers to connect ideas, and designing a coherent structure for a writing piece.
Drafting - working independently to draft the sentence, essay or paper.
Revising - editing based on structure tone and clear connections.

> **Quick Tip:**
> A **peer review** is when teachers encourage students to read over each other's papers for content and understanding. Students provide feedback to each other.

Editing - editing based conventions and proofing from the teacher review or peer review. You can model reading your own writing and do a think aloud about how you could add more details and make it clearer.

Rewriting - incorporating changes as they carefully write or type their final drafts.

Publishing - producing and disseminating the work in a variety of ways, such as a class book, bulletin board, letters to the editor, school newsletter, or website.

Strategies for the writing process

Mapping sentences or **diagramming** sentences is when students outline the structure of the sentence, which can help students make sure each piece of the sentence is grammatically correct. It can also and give the student a deeper understanding of the English Language.

Teachers use **rubrics** to make expectations and grading procedures clear, and provide a formative assessment to guide and improve your instruction. Rubrics are then used as a final assessment tool.

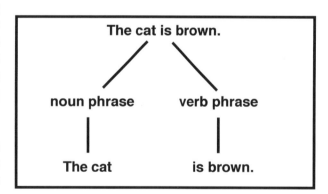

Scenario: After giving a formative assessment, Ms. Jones notices her students are having trouble writing correct sentences. She wants to give them practice so they can write better. She decides to have students map sentences so they can understand the structure. This is considered a **syntactic analysis.**

Example Rubric

	1 - Minimal	2 - Meets	3 - Exceeds
Mechanics (Syntactic)	Many spelling, grammar, and punctuation errors; sentence fragments; incorrect use of capitalization.	Some spelling and grammar errors; most sentences have punctuation and are complete; uses upper- and lowercase letters.	Correct spelling, grammar, and punctuation; complete sentences; correct use of capitalization.
Ideas and Content (Semantic)	Key words are not near the beginning; no clear topic; no beginning, middle, and end; ideas are not ordered.	Main idea or topic is in first sentence; semi-defined topic; attempts beginning, middle and end sections; some order of main idea and details in sequence.	Interesting, well-stated main idea or topic sentence; uses logical plan with an effective beginning, middle, and end; good flow of ideas from topic sentence to details in sequence.
Organization	Very unorganized and confusing.	Organized enough to read and understand the ideas.	Very organized and easy to understand.

Modes of Writing

Modes of writing are the variety, conventions, and purposes of the major kinds of language-based communication, particularly writing and speaking. Four of the most common modes of writing are narrative, descriptive, expository, and persuasive.

Descriptive - writing that describes or helps form a visual picture using sensory details and spacial order.

Narrative - a first person account that tells a story as it happens using sensory details and chronological order.

Expository/Informative Expository - writing that informs, explains, or tells "how to" without using opinions (just the facts).

Persuasive - writing that persuades or convinces using support, details, and examples from the text in logical order (most important to least or least important to most). In early grades this is called *opinion writing*.

> **Quick Tip:** Selecting the correct mode for the appropriate occasion and audience is key. Students should understand which mode to use based on what they are trying to say and who they are trying to say it to.

Instructional Methods for Writing

Instructional methods for writing include producing picture books, recipes, brochures, essays, social studies reports, movie reviews, web site reviews, letters to the editor, book reviews, memoirs.

Emphasis on revision – revising pieces thoughtfully over time—not a new piece of writing each day (much writing will not leave draft form).

Conference/assessment notes – keeping a log or portfolio on each student's writing progress.

Spelling and vocabulary – connecting both to writing, reading and language use.

Sentence structure and conventions – practicing in context, using mini-lessons, not isolated skills sheets.

Meaningful feedback - providing students with specific details as you review their work.

Quick Tip: Communicating expectations is key. Be sure to use rubrics and allow students to use those rubrics before they begin the writing process and as they are writing.

Competency 4: Knowledge of literary instruction and assessments

1. Distinguish among different types of assessments (e.g., norm-referenced, criterion-referenced, diagnostic, curriculum-based) and their purposes and characteristics.
2. Select and apply oral and written methods for assessing student progress (e.g., informal reading inventories, fluency checks, rubrics, story retelling, portfolios).
3. Analyze assessment data (e.g., screening, progress monitoring, diagnostic) to guide instructional decisions and differentiate instruction.
4. Analyze and interpret students' formal and informal assessment results to inform students and stakeholders.
5. Evaluate the appropriateness of assessment instruments and practices.
6. Select appropriate classroom organizational formats (e.g., literature circles, small groups, individuals, workshops, reading centers, multiage groups) for specific instructional objectives.
7. Evaluate methods for the diagnosis, prevention, and intervention of common emergent literacy difficulties.

Assessment Types

There are several different types of assessments educators can use to gauge student learning, inform instruction, and make decisions about students' academic careers.

Assessment Type	Defintion	Example
Diagnostic	A pre-assessment providing instructors with information about students' prior knowledge, **preconceptions,** and **misconceptions before** beginning a learning activity.	Before starting a unit on earth space science, a teacher gives a quick assessment to determine students knowledge, perceptions and misconceptions about earth space science.
Formative	A range of formal and informal assessments or checks conducted by the teacher before during and after learning process in order to modify instruction.	A teacher walks around the room checking on students as they read. She might also write anecdotal notes to review later to help her design further instruction.
Summative	An assessment that focuses on the outcome of a program or lesson.	Midterms, Finals, FSA, EOC.
Criterion Referenced	An assessment that measures student performance against a fixed set of predetermined criteria or learning standards.	The FCAT, EOC, and FSA are criterion reference tests.
Norm-reference	An assessment, or evaluation which yields an estimate of the position of the tested individual in a predefined population with respect to the trait being measured.	The NAEP is an exam given every few years for data purposes only to compare students reading scores across the U.S.

Assessing Student Progress

Assessing student progress is an important component of teaching. Teachers can use an infinite amount of different strategies to monitor and assess student achievement.

Informal assessments, sometimes referred to as **formative** assessments and **alternative** assessments, are a great way to understand student progress. With informal assessments teachers can target students' specific problem areas, adapt instruction, and intervene earlier rather than later.

Types of Informal Assessments

- **Oral assessments** - Assessments that are conducted, either wholly or in part, by word of mouth. Oral assessments include:
    - Answering questions orally.
    - Performances.
    - Presentations.
    - Role play

> **Quick Tip:** Teachers often use oral assessments when working with English language learners (ELL). It is easier for students who speak another language to communicate through oral assessments.

- **Written Assessments** - Assessments where students write to communicate their learning. Written assessments often yield more information than a multiple choice test. Teachers should use rubrics to written assessments. Written assessments include:
    - essays
    - lab Write Up
    - letters
    - journals
- **Performance-Based** - Assessments where students are required to solve problems demonstrating their knowledge and skills. Anytime a student has to perform a task rather than simply fill in multiple choice bubbles, is a performances-based assessment. Performance-based assessments are considered **authentic assessments** and include:
    - participating in a lab or experiment.
    - solving and showing work for math problems.
    - engaging in role play.
    - conducting a presentation.
    - building picture books.
- **Portfolios** - Assessments where the teacher uses a series of student-developed artifacts to determine student learning. Portfolios are considered a form of **authentic** assessment and **alternative** assessment. Portfolios offer an **alternative** or an addition to traditional methods of grading and high stakes exams.

> **Scenario:** Mr. Rodriguez is sitting down with a third grade student as they look over the work the student has done over the last quarter. Mr. Rodriguez and his student then discuss short-term and long-term goals, and a plan to reach those goals based on the data. They are progress monitoring using a portfolio review/assessment.

Progress monitoring should be a component of student learning and assessment. Progress monitoring is when the teacher and the student track progress and modify instruction and behaviors to increase student learning. Students and teachers can progress monitor through a variety of ways including:

- data folders
- fluency checks
- portfolios
- conferences

Differentiated Instruction

Differentiated instruction is providing students with multiple ways to learn in the same classroom. Because classrooms are full of students from various backgrounds and abilities, teachers cannot teach one way and expect to reach all students. Using assessment data and observations, a teacher can provide different materials, instruction and assessments to meet the needs of every student. Differentiated instruction includes:

- providing ELL students a Spanish-to-English dictionary during a vocabulary lesson.
- distributing different reading tasks based on student reading strengths and weaknesses.
- conferencing with high-achieving and struggling students to craft instruction to meet their individual needs.

Classroom instructional/organizational formats
To differentiate instruction and meet the needs of every student, teachers can chose from a variety of different instructional and organizational formats.

Cooperative learning - small teams of students (3-5), each with students of different levels of ability. Use a variety of learning activities to improve their understanding of a subject.

Cooperative learning includes:
- literature circles.
- workshops.
- reading centers.
- discussion grous.

Classroom Set-Up
The way teachers set up their classrooms is essential for effective differentiated instruction to take place. Teachers should organize their classrooms in a way that promotes cooperative learning. Classrooms should also be organized so there is a natural flow for traffic. Teachers can ensure effective classroom organization by:

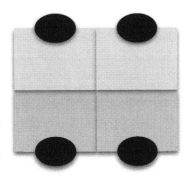

Group desk arrangement for cooperative learning.

- Arranging desks in group formations of 3-5. (Just say no to rows!)
  - This is helpful for literature circles, group discussions, and workshops.
- Noticing student traffic patterns and arranging desks accordingly.
  - This is helpful when a teacher sees that students bump into each other or knock over items on other students' desks when getting up to sharpen pencils, grab reading books, or go to the bathroom.
- Eliminating clutter and unnecessary items that may impede classroom flow.
  - This is helpful so students have an open, clean space to learn. Clutter can freak students out.

Scenario: Because she has students of all reading levels as well as students who are ELLs, Ms. Jimenez decides to use cooperative learning in the form of literature circles. She assigns each student in each group a task based on ability. Students are encouraged to demonstrate learning in a variety of ways: writing, speaking, listening and drawing. Ms. Jimenez is using differentiated instruction effectively.

Methods for Diagnosis, Prevention and Intervention

Teachers must use a variety of information to diagnose student learning and make decisions regarding effective instruction based on that diagnosis. Teachers do this by looking at various data points throughout the year. Data can be obtained through test scores, as well as formative assessments such as running records, fluency checks, and observations.

Interpreting Data

The assessment used in Florida schools to assess students ELA and Reading is the FSA. Students scores range from 1-5, 1 being the lowest and 5 being the highest.

Reading Achievement Levels	
Level 5	This student is above grade level and can easily answer complex questions.
Level 4	This student is at and slightly above grade level and can answer most of the test questions correctly and has a little bit of success with complex problems.
Level 3	This student is reading on grade level but needs help with complex questions.
Level 2	This student has some success on reading assessments but is reading slightly below grade level and cannot answer complex questions.
Level 1	This student has little success on reading assessments and is reading below grade level.

Students who are **level 1 and 2** readers need interventions in the form of intensive reading instruction.

Students who are **level 3** readers are often called "bubble kids" when they are low level 3s because they are at risk of falling to the level 2. To ensure they stay at a 3 or improve to a 4, teachers should monitor these students closely and provide them with challenging reading opportunities.

Students who are a **level 4 or 5** must be challenged daily so they maintain those proficiency levels.

A **stanine** score is a method of scaling test scores on a 9 point standard scale with a mean of 5 and a standard deviation of 2.

1, 2, or 3 is below average.
4, 5, or 6 is average.
7, 8, or 9 is above average.

Scenario: If a student scores a level 3 on the ELA FSA and has a stanine of 7, that student should stay on level and even be challenged with complex text slightly beyond her level.

Competency 5: Knowledge of communication and media literacy

1. Identify characteristics of penmanship (e.g., legibility, letter formation, spacing).
2. Distinguish among listening and speaking strategies (e.g., questioning, paraphrasing, eye contact, voice, gestures).
3. Identify and apply instructional methods (e.g., collaborative conversation, collaborative discussion, presentation) for developing listening and speaking skills.
4. Select and evaluate a wide array of resources (e.g., Internet, printed material, artifacts, visual media, primary sources) for research and presentation.
5. Determine and apply the ethical process (e.g., citation, paraphrasing) for collecting and presenting authentic information while avoiding plagiarism.
6. Identify and evaluate current technology for use in educational settings.

Penmanship

Teaching handwriting or penmanship is important; teachers can learn a lot about students while looking at their penmanship. Teaching penmanship should include:

- consistency
- motor pattern
- similarly formed letters
- separate reversible letters (b and d)
- integration of letter formation to letter sounds

Assessment of handwriting should incorporate observations of **execution, legibility, and speed** of writing.

Speaking and Listening

Assessing speaking and listening skills in the classroom is essential in teaching students to read and write. Reading, writing, speaking and listening all go together.

Ways teachers can teach speaking and listening skills is to ask students to:
- Paraphrase what they just read. This is also effective in reading instruction.
- Ask questions. Asking questions helps with comprehension too.
- Use voice inflections when cued by punctuation and grammar.

Group discussions, debates, and collaborative dialogue also help teachers reinforce speaking and listening skills.

Media

Teachers have access to a variety of media resources to enhance classroom instruction. These resources include media centers and computer labs. Teachers must choose wisely and train students how to use these resources wisely.

The **internet** is an amazing tool for searching lots of information. Students should be instructed to discern between accurate information and inaccurate information.

Teachers should also use a variety of primary and secondary resources.

	Humanities	Sciences
Primary Sources	• diaries, journals, and letters • interviews with people who lived during a particular time (e.g., survivors of genocide in Rwanda or in the Holocaust.) • songs, plays, novels, stories • paintings, drawings, and sculptures	• published results of research studies • published results of scientific experiments • published results of clinical trials • proceedings of conferences and meetings
Secondary Sources	• biographies • histories • literary criticism • book, art, and theater reviews • newspaper articles that interpret	• publications about the significance of research or experiments • analysis of a clinical trial • review of the results of several experiments or trials

Citing Sources - The Common Core Standards have pushed for more text-based evidence in discussions and writing. That means students must use evidence from the text to support their claims. Therefore, teachers must be vigilant about plagiarism. In addition, teachers should provide expectations and assistance when it comes to properly citing primary and secondary sources for research, book reports, presentations, and more.

Technology

Technology should enhance the learning experience. Teachers have the opportunity to use a variety of different technologies in the classroom. Whatever technology teachers choose, it should be age-appropriate, meaning it shouldn't be too complex for young learners or too easy for advanced learners. Technology should also reflect the task students are being asked to perform.

Textbooks vs Computers

Textbook Pros	Computer Pros
Students are able to use something tangible. No matter how amazing technology gets, students still love physical books.	The computer can increase the question complexity when a student begins to answer questions correctly.
Students can read text in physical books more easily than they can read on computers.	The computer can store a million textbooks in its memory.

Practice Test

1. The first developmental phase in reading is:

    A. emergent

    B. early

    C. fluent

    D. transitional

2. Which statement is NOT true about emergent readers?

    A. They hear individual sounds in words.

    B. They use illustrations to extract meaning.

    C. They read without pointing to individual words.

    D. They recognize letters in their own name

3. Which type of formative assessment is NOT utilized in the scenario below?

    Ms. Lopez administers an oral reading fluency assessment to Marisa. While Marisa reads, Ms. Lopez marks errors on her copy of the text and also notes the words Marisa says in place of the correct word(s). After the assessment, Ms. Lopez examines her records in order to identify the type(s) of errors Marisa made in order to determine the next step in reading instruction.

    A. running records

    B. silent reading comprehension

    C. miscue analysis

    D. oral fluency check

4. After a guided reading activity, Mr. Jackson asks his 4th grade students to divide any compound words found in the text. This student activity is an example of:

    A. phonic analysis.

    B. blending.

    C. rhyming.

    D. structural analysis.

5. Which is the best instructional strategy for developing concepts of print?

    A. readers theater

    B. silent sustained reading

    C. shared reading

    D. oral reading fluency

6. Mr. Skinner's students are breaking down word parts to better understand their meaning.

   Which instructional strategy is Mr. Skinner using?

   A. structural analysis

   B. phonemic analysis

   C. clapping syllables

   D. interactive writing

7. Read the scenario below and answer the question that follows.

   Mrs. Diaz implements readers theater into her 3rd grade class. This activity involves reading parts from a text.

   What does this strategy help to build?

   A. vocabulary

   B. comprehension

   C. fluency

   D. phonological awareness

8. How is differentiated instruction different from accommodations?

   A. Differentiated instruction is a way to meet the needs of students with differing abilities in the same class while accommodations modify the curriculum and student expectations in order to ensure student learning gains.

   B. Differentiated instruction focuses on reducing the effects of a student's learning disability through modified activities while accommodations are used to help the teacher meet the needs of all the students in his or her classroom through one learning activity.

   C. Differentiated instruction focuses solely on varying activities so each student can learn at his or her own pace while accommodations focus on the supports a student needs to be successful in the general curriculum.

   D. Differentiated instruction provides alternatives for students to learn the same material based on readiness, interests, and learning needs while accommodations reduce the effects of a learning disability without decreasing learning expectations.

9. Which is NOT an example of figurative language?

    A. simile

    B. idiom

    C. anecdote

    D. onomatopoeia

10. When a student has awareness of phonemes in words, syllables, onset-rime segments, and spelling he or she is demonstrating:

    A. phonological awareness.

    B. phonics mastery.

    C. phonemic awareness.

    D. structural analysis.

11. Which is NOT an appropriate written language skill for a student to master by the end of 3rd grade?

    A. provide a concluding statement or section

    B. provide references for cited text

    C. provide reasons that support an opinion

    D. develop a topic with facts, definitions, and details

12. Which is NOT an important component of fluency?

    A. use context to confirm or self-correct word recognition and understanding

    B. read on-level text with purpose and understanding

    C. read on-level text orally with accuracy, appropriate rate, and expression

    D. use morphology to read unfamiliar multisyllabic words in context

13. Which of the following is effective in building fluency and confidence?

    A. choral reading

    B. echo reading

    C. round robin reading

    D. literature circles

14. During a modeled writing activity, the students are primarily:

    A. copying the teacher's writing.

    B. listening and watching.

    C. engaging in internal dialogue.

    D. independently applying targeted skills.

15. Which assessment method would be appropriate to guide instruction for fluency issues?

      A. informal reading inventory

      B. readers theater

      C. multiple choice test

      D. spelling quiz

16. Choral poetry positively impacts which of the following reading skills?

      A. inference, fluency, vocabulary

      B. stamina, inference, comprehension

      C. fluency, inference, vocabulary

      D. fluency, vocabulary, comprehension

17. Which is the most appropriate use of anecdotal notes?

      A. as a list all of the behavioral issues a student exhibits while in the classroom

      B. as evidence during parent-teacher conference for discipline measures taken

      C. as an objective record of student behaviors and/or learning to guide classroom practices

      D. provide an ongoing record for the student portfolio to help determine retention

18. Mr. Adams' 4th grade class is engaging in narrative writing through a personal memory essay. One of the activities includes a peer review.

During which part the of 5-step writing process would this occur?

      A. after pre-writing/before drafting

      B. after revision/before editing

      C. after editing/before publishing

      D. after drafting/before revision

19. Which is NOT an appropriate use of a rubric?

      A. to identify miscues in student writing

      B. as a guide and self-evaluation tool for students

      C. as a teacher evaluation tool for student work for an assignment

      D. to set the expectations and criteria for a specific assignment

20. Phonemic awareness includes the ability to:

    A. form compound words and combine word parts.

    B. spell accurately and decode unfamiliar words.

    C. pronounce individual sounds in words.

    D. differentiate between homonyms and spell accurately.

21. Which is NOT a best practice for vocabulary instruction?

    A. model using context clues

    B. teaching prefixes, suffixes and roots

    C. explicit instruction using a dictionary

    D. using word walls for target vocabulary

22. Which of the following are essential skills in reading comprehension?

    A. decoding, spelling, word knowledge

    B. decoding, word recognition, fluency

    C. spelling, fluency, understanding the text

    D. decoding, monitoring, speed

23. To develop phonics skills, students must have which of the following?

    A. graphophonemic knowledge and sight word recognition

    B. decoding skills and reading fluency

    C. decoding skills and graphophonemic knowledge

    D. reading fluency and comprehension skills

24. Read the scenario below and answer the question that follows.

    To measure her students' mastery of grade-level presentation skills, which project would be the most appropriate for Mrs. Jones to choose for her 3rd grade students?

    A. a poster with explanations

    B. an oral report with visuals

    C. a travel brochure with visuals

    D. a typed report with citations

25. Read the scenario below and answer the question that follows.

    Mr. Madison is a 5th grade teacher who wants to measure his students' mastery of persuasive writing.

    Which activity would be the most appropriate to meet the objective?

    A. an essay arguing an opinion about a topic

    B. a whole-class debate on a controversial topic

    C. a research project about local wildlife

    D. a series of personal mini-memoirs on a theme

26. What is the most appropriate use of a diagnostic assessment?

    A. to determine student grades

    B. to determine areas of strength and weakness

    C. to determine what to reteach

    D. to determine mastery of a skill

27. Mr. Williams creates 6 heterogeneous groups of 4 students who work together during a literacy unit to achieve shared learning goals and complete specific tasks and assignments. Each group is given explicit instructions and each group member has a specific role to ensure that all students contribute.

    This is an example of:

    A. informal cooperative learning

    B. shared learning

    C. co-dependent learning

    D. formal cooperative learning

28. What are the differences between fixed poetic form and free verse poetry?

    A. fixed poetic form is written in metered verse while free verse poetry has no pre established guidelines.

    B. fixed poetic form is elevated in style while free verse poetry is informal and uses colloquial language.

    C. fixed poetic form has strict guidelines for stanzas while free verse is devoid of stanzas.

    D. fixed poetic form serves as a template for composing a poem while free verse poetry has no pre-established guidelines.

29. Which is NOT a convention of epic poetry?

    A. It is a lengthy narrative about a serious or worthy traditional subject.

    B. The diction is formal and dignified and maintains an objective tone.

    C. It takes place in a confined geographical area sometime in the remote past.

    D. The action contains supernatural feats of strength or military prowess.

30. Read the poem by Edward Lear below and answer the question that follows.

    There was an Old Man in a tree,
    Who was horribly bored by a Bee;
    When they said, 'Does it buzz?'
    He replied, 'Yes, it does! It's a regular brute of a Bee!'

    This is an example of:

    A. limerick.

    B. sonnet.

    C. haiku.

    D. free verse

31. Read the poem below and answer the question that follows.

    The blue ocean gleams.

    Shimmering like precious gems.

    An endless treasure.

    This is an example of:

    A. limerick.

    B. sonnet.

    C. haiku.

    D. free verse.

32. **Juliet is the sun** is an example of which figurative language device?

    A. simile

    B. metaphor

    C. personification

    D. analogy

33. Select the correct order of the first four stages of writing.

    A. wavy scribble, mock letters, scribbling, conventional letters

    B. mock letters, scribbling, wavy scribble, conventional letters

    C. scribbling, mock letters, wavy scribble, conventional letters

    D. scribbling, wavy scribble, mock letters, conventional letters

34. Which is NOT true of the conventional letters stage of writing?

    A. The writing is usually more vertical than horizontal.

    B. The letters are usually from the child's name.

    C. Children are not always conscious they are making conventional letters.

    D. Children often create strings of letters across a page.

35. Which is true of phonetic spelling?

    A. Beginning sounds are used first, middle sounds are used second, followed by ending sounds and vowel sounds.

    B. Beginning sounds are used first, ending sounds are used second, followed by middle sounds and vowel sounds.

    C. Middle sounds are used first, vowel sounds are used second, followed by beginning sounds and ending sounds.

    D. Vowel sounds are used first, followed by beginning sounds, middle sounds, and ending sounds.

36. Which is NOT a characteristic of emergent writing?

    A. conventional spelling

    B. conventional letters

    C. mock letters

    D. inventive spelling

37. Read the scenario below and answer the question that follows.

Trina is a 1st grade student who can read words by remembering visual or contextual cues. She recognizes and read signs and labels in her school and home environments, but cannot read these words when they are shown in isolation. She also lacks the ability to match letters to sounds.

What phase of word recognition is Trina demonstrating?

    A. full-alphabetic

    B. pre-alphabetic

    C. partial-alphabetic

    D. consolidated-alphabetic

38. Read the scenario below and answer the question that follows.

Mr. Lapeer is a new 1st grade teacher who is building his classroom library. Many of his students come from diverse cultural backgrounds where English is the second language used. While the most common second language is Spanish, he also has students whose families speak German and Haitian Creole.

Which type of books would Mr. Lapeer NOT include in his library?

   A. books that are illustrated with exaggerated features of a cultural group

   B. books that portray female characters who break cultural stereotypes

   C. books that portray men of color as positive role models

   D. books that who children with disabilities as capable main characters

39. Which is NOT a characteristic of a reading response journal?

   A. requires students to use background knowledge to construct personal meaning

   B. increases reading level by encouraging students to read complex text

   C. increases comprehension as students integrate new experiences with past ones

   D. increases ability to communicate and refine ideas

40. Which mode of writing tells a story using sequenced events and descriptive details?

   A. expository/explanatory

   B. persuasive

   C. opinion/argumentative

   D. narrative

41. Which is NOT a characteristic of a fable?

   A. anthropomorphized inanimate objects

   B. mythical creatures

   C. exaggerated version of historical events

   D. contains a moral message

42. Which does NOT contribute to legible handwriting?

   A. spacing

   B. block letters

   C. letter formation

   D. letter alignment

43. Which is NOT an appropriate strategy to use when looking for reader response to literature?

    A. choral reading

    B. literature circles

    C. think-pair-share

    D. journals

44. Writing that uses sensory details is:

    A. informational.

    B. expository.

    C. fictional.

    D. descriptive.

45. Read the scenario below and answer the question that follows.

    Most of Ms. Adams' kindergarten students can label pictures in their daily journals with strings of random letters.

What should Ms. Adams' next step be to develop writing skills in those students?

    A. Have the students write short paragraphs about what they have drawn.

    B. Ask the students to engage in peer discussions about their writing.

    C. Ask the students to label their drawings with appropriate initial letters.

    D. Have the students look up the words that match their drawings in a dictionary.

46. Which is NOT a benefit of the workshop approach in the classroom?

    A. It allows adequate time for student practice.

    B. It requires students to learn skills independently.

    C. It allows the teacher to remediate with small groups.

    D. It provides differentiated learning opportunities.

47. Classroom structures should include _____ to allow for multiple speaking and listening opportunities.

    A. formal cooperative learning groups only

    B. informal cooperative learning groups only

    C. a combination of independent and group work

    D. whole group lessons combined with small group lessons

48. Which is NOT an important consideration when setting up the classroom?

    A. the number of students in the class

    B. spacing of the work centers

    C. electrical outlets

    D. a quiet space for independent work

49. When students are asked to use facts and data in their essays in order to inform the reader, they are engaging in _____ writing.

    A. explanatory/expository

    B. persuasive/opinion

    C. descriptive

    D. narrative

50. Which cooperative grouping strategy requires a student to become an expert on a topic and then share the information with peers?

    A. think-pair-share

    B. numbered heads together

    C. jigsaw

    D. rally robin

51. The ELA Florida Standards Assessments (FSA) is an example of a:

    A. diagnostic assessment.

    B. criterion-referenced assessment.

    C. norm-referenced assessment.

    D. formative assessment.

52. Read the scenario below and answer the question that follows.

    Students are taking an exam that will measure their performance against other students in the nation. This is used to make decisions about education programs.

    This type of assessment is:

    A. norm-reference

    B. criterion-reference

    C. summative

    D. formative

53. What is the main purpose of formative assessments?

    A. to be used as grades

    B. to diagnose learning issues

    C. to drive instruction

    D. to used in professional learning communities (PLCs)

54. The STAR Early Literacy Assessment given at the beginning of 2nd grade is an example of:

    A. a diagnostic assessment

    B. a criterion-referenced assessment

    C. a formative assessment

    D. a summative assessment

55. Read the scenario below and answer the question that follows.

During independent reading time, a student notices the characters in his chapter book exhibit distinct behaviors.

Which story element is the student picking up on?

    A. plot

    B. setting

    C. point of view

    D. characterization

56. Which of the following is an example of an onset-rime segmentation?

    A. class-room

    B. walk-ed

    C. d-og

    D. re-wind

57. When a teacher asks students to make predictions about a text, he or she is fostering the students':

    A. fluency.

    B. comprehension.

    C. prosody.

    D. automaticity.

58. Which of the following is NOT a consonant blend?

    A. bl

    B. sh

    C. cr

    D. at

59. Which is NOT a characteristic of successful technology integration in the classroom?

    A. easily accessible to teacher and students

    B. routinely used

    C. supports curricular goals

    D. independent computer-based learning

60. When the goal is enhanced information and media literacy, which is NOT a consideration?

    A. Who is the main character?

    B. Who is the intended audience?

    C. Who is conveying the message?

    D. What media is used to deliver the message?

Answers - Practice Test ELA

1. A	16. D	31.C	46. B
2. C	17. C	32. B	47. D
3. B	18. D	33. D	48. C
4. D	19. A	34. A	49. A
5. C	20. C	35. B	50. C
6. A	21. C	36. A	51. B
7. C	22. B	37. B	52. A
8. D	23. C	38. A	53. C
9. C	24. B	39. B	54. A
10. A	25. A	40. D	55. D
11. B	26. B	41. B	56. C
12. D	27. D	42. B	57. B
13. A	28. D	43. A	58. D
14. B	29. C	44. D	59. D
15. A	30. A	45. C	60. A

Answer Explanations - ELA

1. **A.** The emergent stage is when children just begin to recognize the relationships between symbols (letters) and the sounds they make. At this stage, students require support in the way of pictures. In other words, they rely heavily on the pictures to get the meaning.

2. **C.** Remember, emergent readers are just beginning to recognize the sound-symbol relationships. One of the signs of an emergent reader is that he/she finger points to words. Fluent readers do not need to point to individual words in a text.

3. **B.** Fluency cannot be measured with silent reading. The scenario described uses running records, miscue analysis, and an oral fluency check.

4. **D.** Structural analysis is when a word is broken down into known parts such as individual words in a compound word or prefix, root, and suffix.

5. **C.** Be careful with these questions. Shared reading has many benefits, including modeling fluency, but the key phrase in this question is *concepts of print*. In shared reading, students focus on the pictures and text, developing their concept of print. They start to make phonemic connections to the symbols for letters. Oral reading fluency measures their ability to read text aloud, and readers theater also builds fluency, so you can eliminate (A) and (D). Silent sustained reading would be done after the student can read independently, not when they are still building concepts of print.

6. **A.** In a structural analysis, the students break words down into their parts such as prefixes, roots, and suffixes, or the two words that form a compound word. Phonemic analysis does not involve print, only sounds, and clapping syllables would be a good phonemic awareness activity.

7. **C.** Readers theater is best for building and supporting fluency. While fluency is an important part of students' comprehension, reading parts aloud from a text is not the best way to measure it.

8. **D.** When dealing with two-part answers, make sure you really look at both parts for any incorrect phrasing. This is the only answer that meets the criteria of defining both differentiated instruction and accommodations correctly. Accommodations do NOT modify the curriculum. The curriculum stays the same, but the student is given supports to meet the same learning goals as his/her peers.

9. **C.** Anecdotes are a great way for an author to make a point in an interesting way, but they do not fall under the figurative language umbrella because they are literal.

10. **A.** All these individual skills fit under the umbrella of phonological awareness. Phonological awareness is a broad set of skills that includes identifying and manipulating units of oral language—parts such as phonemes in words, syllables, and onsets and rimes. Students with phonological awareness also understand conventional spelling. Remember, phonemic awareness is a sub-skill of phonological awareness and only deals with the smallest unit of sound, the phoneme. Signs of strong phonemic awareness include being able to hear rhyme and alliteration. Although they are often used interchangeably, when talking about reading skills, phonological awareness is

usually the correct term.

11. **B.** Students in 3rd grade would not be expected to provide references for cited text. They would be expected to cite textual evidence in written answers.

12. **D.** Using morphology to read words in context is the only one not identified as a component of fluency. Fluency is verbal, and morphology is the study of the forms of words—prefixes, roots, suffixes, plurals, parts of speech—and focuses on written language.

13. **A.** Choral reading provides built-in support for those students who may feel self-conscious reading aloud. During this unison reading, students' fluency is supported as they build
speed, prosody, and accuracy and is a non-threatening, low-risk way for students to practice and build confidence.

14. **B.** The purpose of modeling is to show the students what the expected outcome looks like. They must be actively watching and listening for this to be effective.

15. **A.** This is considered an informal diagnostic assessment, and therefore would be the most appropriate method to use when dealing with reading issues — in this case fluency. Readers theater, although a great way to practice and demonstrate fluency, won't give you the detailed data that an IRI will. A multiple choice test is summative and doesn't measure fluency, and a spelling quiz doesn't measure fluency.

16. **D.** This is the only combo that accurately names the reading skills choral poetry will foster. Students won't gain stamina, eliminating (B). Stamina is gained more through independent reading of complex texts where they learn to focus for longer periods of time. Inferencing requires the student to interpret, make connections, and draw conclusions and is not best supported by choral poetry reading.

17. **C.** Note the phrase *most appropriate*. This means that while there may be some truth to the other answers, your job is to find the best answer. Eliminate (A) because of the word *all*. Anecdotal notes should be targeted on one specific behavior at a time. The word *evidence* in (B) suggests that the child is on trial and is a little too harsh. In addition, anecdotal notes are not solely for behaviors. Using anecdotal notes to determine retention wouldn't be appropriate; portfolios, assessment data, and student growth data would be better. (C) is the best answer because it includes the word *objective* and also has the goal of guiding classroom practices. All the others are too specific.

18. **D.** The five stages in the writing process are: pre-writing, drafting, revising, editing, and publishing. A peer edit would be most appropriate after the drafting stage before the writer makes revisions.

19. **A.** Rubrics are not meant to modify curriculum or learning outcomes. In fact, modifications are huge no-no's except in situations where a child needs specially designed instruction due to a neurological disability. All the other choices fit into the purpose of a rubric, and it is best practice to use a rubric for all three.

20. **C.** Remember, phonemic awareness is a sub-skill of phonological awareness. While the terms are often used synonymously, they are not the same thing. When a

student can recognize and pronounce individual sounds in words, or phonemes, he or she is demonstrating phonemic awareness. The other choices are indicative of phonological awareness.

21. **C.** Using the dictionary to look up words is not an example of effective vocabulary instruction. It's never going to be the answer! Dictionaries are great for confirming working meanings developed from context.

22. **B.** Although spelling seems to make sense, the essential reading skills are decoding, word recognition, and fluency, so eliminate (A) and (C). Speed (rate) is included in fluency, so it's too specific, eliminating (D).

23. **C.** Students must have decoding skills and the ability to match symbols with sounds (graphophonemic knowledge) to develop phonics skills. Fluency is not a necessary skill for phonics, eliminating (B) and (D). Eliminate (A) because the students aren't sounding out sight words.

24. **B.** This includes a presentation by the students. None of the other options specify that the student is presenting his or her project.

25. **A.** This measures an individual student's mastery of persuasive writing. The debate is oral, and the other options do not require persuasive writing.

26. **B.** Diagnostics are used before instruction, making (C) incorrect. (A) and (D) are summative, so eliminate those.

27. **D.** Here, the teacher has created groups with a shared learning goal, specific tasks, and roles for each member. Informal cooperative learning can be pulled off with less planning and to aid to direct instruction. Think group activities to break up a lecture. Shared learning doesn't specify the creation of heterogenous groups, only learning is shared to reach a goal. There is no such thing as co-dependent learning.

28. **D.** Fixed poems have a template. There are many different types, but the idea is the poet fits his or her words into a specific form (think sonnet, haiku, limerick). (A) is the trick answer. Not ALL fixed poems have metered verse. (B) is an example of epic poetry, and (C) assumes free verse poetry doesn't have stanzas, which is not true. It may or may not.

29. **C.** Epic poetry takes place in a large geographical area (think Odyssey & Beowulf). The other choices are conventions of epic poetry.

30. **A.** Limericks have five structured lines of comical/nonsensical content with obvious rhymes. Sonnets have 14 lines of iambic pentameter. English sonnets end with a rhyming couplet; haikus have a specific amount of syllables in each line (5-7-5), and free verse poetry has no set line length, rhythm, or rhyming pattern.

31. **C.** Haikus have a specific amount of syllables in each line (5-7-5).

32. **B.** Metaphors compare two unlike things directly without the use of *like* or *as*. They are often confused with similes, which compare two unlike things but do use *like* or *as*. Personification gives human qualities to things that are not human. Analogies compare two things but explain what they have in common by describing similarities and are not technically figurative language.

33. **D.** Knowing the order of the seven developmental stages of writing, along with the characteristics of each, is a must for this test: scribbling, wavy scribble, mock letters,

conventional letters, invented spelling, approximated spelling, and conventional spelling.

34. **A.** This is characteristic of the mock letters stage.

35. **B.** This follows the pattern of how sounds students learn sounds.

36. **A.** Conventional spelling is NOT a characteristic of an emergent writer. That comes when the student enters the fluent stage of writing.

37. **B.** Children at this stage memorize the visual features of words and can guess them in context/environmental print. However, when the words are shown to the child without the environmental cues, they cannot read the word because he or she has not made the necessary connections between the phonemes and graphemes. In full alphabetic (A), children can decode unfamiliar words and store sight words in memory. In partial alphabetic (C), children recognize some letter-sound connections and can use them in context to remember words by sight. In consolidated alphabetic (D), children recognize larger units of blended sound that recur in different words.

38. **A.** Sounds like common sense, but it is trickier than you may think. Just be very careful of illustrations and make sure that any portrayal of characters shows that the person is capable and serves as a positive role model.

39. **B.** Although reading response journals do result in a confidence boost that increases motivation to read, the phrases *increases reading level* and *complex text* make this particular choice correct.

40. **D.** Narratives always tell a story; explanatory (formerly expository) writing explains, persuasive (called argumentative in upper grades and opinion in lower grades) aims to assert a point with the intention of getting others to agree.

41. **B.** Myths have mythical creatures. Myths, fables, and folk tales often get confused, so it's worth knowing the characteristics of each.

42. **B.** Legible handwriting doesn't have to contain block letters. The other three choices are features of legible handwriting.

43. **A.** Choral, or unison, reading does not involve students' response to the literature. The other choices do.

44. **D.** Sensory details can be used in other types of writing, but descriptive writing **must** have sensory details (sights, sounds, colors, etc.).

45. **C.** This makes the most sense to continue to develop skills. They are not ready for paragraphs, peer discussions won't meet the goal, and dictionaries are never the answer!

46. **B.** Workshops are geared more toward peer/collaborative work while the teacher leads small group or individual instruction.

47. **D.** The word *multiple* is key. (A) and (B) both have the qualifier, *only*, so eliminate those. Independent work doesn't allow for speaking and listening, so (C) is also out.

48. **C.** Remember, seating arrangements need to encourage active participation and provide the best learning environment for the students. While it may be ideal to have a computer center near electrical outlets, it is not the most pressing consideration.

49. **A.** This kind of writing informs or explains something to the reader.

50. **C.** In a jigsaw, the text is broken into chunks. Each student from a group is assigned a different chunk of the text to read and report back to the group. It helps improve listening, communication, and problem-solving skills and is also great for student engagement when tackling longer texts.

51. **B.** Because it is based on standards, the FSA is criterion referenced (criteria=standards).

52. **A.** Norm-referenced tests measure how a student compares to his or her peers.

53. **C.** Formative assessments don't diagnose, they should not be used as grades, and although the results can be discussed at PLCs, that is not the MAIN goal. The main purpose is to inform and drive future instruction.

54. **A.** The STAR Early Literacy test is a diagnostic for reading skills. It is not criterion-referenced because it is not intended to measure mastery of standards, or criteria. Formative (C) is used after a diagnostic and instruction to monitor progress and drive further instruction. Summative (D) is a "final" test to measure mastery of standards.

55. **D.** This literary device is when the author shows the characters' motivations and personality. The plot (A) details the main events in the story, the setting (B) is where the story takes place, and point of view (C) is the perspective from which the story is told.

56. **C.** The other choices are examples of structural analysis.

57. **B.** Prosody and automaticity are components of fluency, so you can eliminate all three of these choices.

58. **D.** This is the only choice that is a combination of a vowel and consonant.

59. **D.** This is not one of the identified characteristics of technology integration. The word *independent* sets it apart from the others. It's not always appropriate for children to work independently. While students can and most likely will work independently. on computers, technology integration encompasses more than that.

60. **A.** In media literacy, the message, audience, and delivery method are the main considerations. Who is at the center of the story is not.

Additional Practice - ELA

An important skill in slaying the test, is the ability to transfer knowledge from one area to another. That way, no matter how the questions are worded, you have the transfer skills and the flexible thinking to answer accurately. We find that writing your own items for each sub-skill on the test is a great way to sharpen your transfer skills. When you write your own test questions while studying, you're thinking like a test maker and not a test taker!

The following pages provide you an opportunity to write your own test questions for each competency and its sub-skills.

Competency 1 - Knowledge of the reading process

sub-skill	test question	answer choices
Identify the content of emergent literacy (e.g., oral language development, phonological awareness, alphabet knowledge, decoding, concepts of print, motivation, text structures, written language development).		
Identify the processes, skills, and stages of word recognition that lead to effective decoding (e.g., pre-alphabetic, partial-alphabetic, full-alphabetic, graphophonemic, morphemic).		
Select and apply instructional methods for the development of decoding skills (e.g., continuous blending, chunking).		
Distinguish among the components of reading fluency (e.g., accuracy,automaticity, rate, prosody).		
Choose and apply instructional methods for developing reading fluency (e.g., practice with high-frequency words, readers theatre, repeated readings).		
Identify and differentiate instructional methods and strategies for increasing vocabulary acquisition across the content areas (e.g., word analysis, author's word choice, context clues, multiple exposures).		

Identify and evaluate instructional methods and strategies for facilitating students' reading comprehension (e.g., summarizing, self-monitoring, questioning, use of graphic and semantic organizers, think alouds, recognizing story structure).		
Identify essential comprehension skills (e.g., main idea, supporting details and facts, author's purpose, point of view, inference, conclusion).		
Determine appropriate uses of multiple representations of information for a variety of purposes (e.g., charts, tables, graphs, pictures, print and nonprint media).		
Determine and analyze strategies for developing critical-thinking skills such as analysis, synthesis, and evaluation (e.g., making connections and predictions, questioning, summarizing, question generating).		
Evaluate and select appropriate instructional strategies for teaching a variety of informational and literary text.		
Identify the content of emergent literacy (e.g., oral language development, phonological awareness, alphabet knowledge, decoding, concepts of print, motivation, text structures, written language development).		
Identify the processes, skills, and stages of word recognition that lead to effective decoding (e.g., pre-alphabetic, partial-alphabetic, full-alphabetic, graphophonemic, morphemic).		

Competency 2 - Knowledge of literary analysis and genres

sub-skill	test question	answer choices
Differentiate among characteristics and elements of a variety of literary genres (e.g., realistic fiction, fantasy, poetry, informational texts).		
Identify and analyze terminology and intentional use of literary devices (e.g., simile, metaphor, personification, onomatopoeia, hyperbole).		
Evaluate and select appropriate multicultural texts based on purpose, relevance, cultural sensitivity, and developmental appropriateness.		
Identify and evaluate appropriate techniques for varying student response to texts (e.g., think-pair-share, reading response journals, evidence-based discussion).		

Competency 3 - Knowledge of language and the writing process.

sub-skill	test question	answer choices
Identify and evaluate the developmental stages of writing (e.g., drawing, dictating, writing).		
Differentiate stages of the writing process (i.e., prewriting, drafting, revising, editing, publishing).		
Distinguish among the modes of writing (e.g., narrative,informative/ explanatory, argument).		
Select the appropriate mode of writing for a variety of occasions, purposes, and audiences.		
Identify and apply instructional methods for teaching writing conventions (e.g., spelling, punctuation, capitalization, syntax, word usage).		
Apply instructional methods for teaching writer's craft across genres (e.g., precise language, figurative language, linking words, temporal words, dialogue, sentence variety).		

Competency 4 - Knowledge of literary instruction and assessments

sub-skill	test question	answer choices
Distinguish among different types of assessments (e.g., norm-referenced, criterion-referenced, diagnostic, curriculum-based) and their purposes and characteristics.		
Select and apply oral and written methods for assessing student progress (e.g., informal reading inventories, fluency checks, rubrics, story retelling, portfolios).		
Analyze assessment data (e.g., screening, progress monitoring, diagnostic) to guide instructional decisions and differentiate instruction.		
Analyze and interpret students' formal and informal assessment results to inform students and stakeholders.		
Evaluate the appropriateness of assessment instruments and practices.		
Select appropriate classroom organizational formats (e.g., literature circles, small groups, individuals, workshops, reading centers, multiage groups) for specific instructional objectives.		
Evaluate methods for the diagnosis, prevention, and intervention of common emergent literacy difficulties.		
Distinguish among different types of assessments (e.g., norm-referenced, criterion-referenced, diagnostic, curriculum-based) and their purposes and characteristics.		
Select and apply oral and written methods for assessing student progress (e.g., informal reading inventories, fluency checks, rubrics, story retelling, portfolios).		

Competency 5 - Knowledge of communication and media literacy

sub-skill	test question	answer choices
Identify characteristics of penmanship (e.g., legibility, letter formation, spacing).		
Distinguish among listening and speaking strategies (e.g., questioning, paraphrasing, eye contact, voice, gestures).		
Identify and apply instructional methods (e.g., collaborative conversation, collaborative discussion, presentation) for developing listening and speaking skills.		
Select and evaluate a wide array of resources (e.g., Internet, printed material, artifacts, visual media, primary sources) for research and presentation.		
Determine and apply the ethical process (e.g., citation, paraphrasing) for collecting and presenting authentic information while avoiding plagiarism.		
Identify and evaluate current technology for use in educational settings.		

This page is intentionally left blank.

II. Social Science

This chapter provides an overview of the competencies for the social science section of Elementary ED (K-6) Subject Area Exam. This section has explanations regarding all the competencies tested on the exam as well as in depth analysis of the types of questions students will encounter when taking this test.

The competencies addressed in this chapter are from the Florida Teacher Certification Examination Test Information Guide.

You can access that using this link:
http://www.fl.nesinc.com/PDFs/ElemEd_K-6_TIG_4thEd_DOE040115.pdf)

Competency 1: Knowledge of effective instructional practices and assessment

1. Select appropriate resources for instructional delivery of social science concepts, including complex informational text.
2. Identify appropriate resources for planning for instruction of social science concepts.
3. Choose appropriate methods for assessing social science concepts.
4. Determine appropriate learning environments for social science lessons.

Teaching & Assessment

Criterion-referenced tests are designed to measure student performance against a fixed set of predetermined criteria or learning standards. Criterion-referenced assessments include:

- FSA
- SAT 10
- FCAT

Norm-referenced tests report whether test takers performed better or worse than a hypothetical average student, which is determined by comparing scores against the performance results of a statistically selected group of test takers, typically of the same age or grade level, who have already taken the exam. Norm-referenced assessments include:

- Iowa Basic Skills Test
- National Reading Test (NRT)

Writing in the Social Science Content Area
Rubrics are used to let students know the expectations for an assignment. Rubrics are typically used in writing, but they can be used for any project. In social science rubrics should contain attributes for social science content and ELA grammar and mechanics.

Cooperative Learning
Social science instruction can be enhanced when teachers use cooperative learning strategies. Cooperative learning is effective when it is well-planned and every student plays a significant role in the learning process. Types of cooperative learning include:

Literature Circles

Literature circles are well-organized cooperative learning structures where students analyze text, both informational and literary. The characteristics include:

- Involve high expectations and rigor.
- Require individual student participation that contributes to the group.
  - Every student has a role (administrator, reader, notetaker, organizer, etc).
- Reader response centered and focused on student independence and ownership.
- Involve various types of assessment (including self-assessment, observations and conferences)

> **Scenario:**
>
> Literature circles can be used effectively for a students learning about the language in the Declaration of Independence.

Debates

When students participate in debates, either as a group or as individuals, they have an opportunity to use critical thinking and presentation skills. Debates help students cultivate abstract thinking and build skills like citizenship, etiquette, organization, persuasion, public speaking, research, and teamwork.

Role Play

Role play can be use to enhance students' understanding of a situation in time. Role playing is most effectively used when demonstrating a cast of characters in a certain event.

> **Scenario**:
>
> Examples of when role play would be appropriate in a classroom include:
> - the Battle of Bunker Hill.
> - the signing of the Declaration of Independence.

Technology

Technology will never replace the teacher. Furthermore, good tech will never make up for bad teaching. However, it *can* enhance the classroom experience for students. Use technology in social science to broaden students' experiences:

- virtual tours of ancient cities
- Google for information on a broad range of topics.

Primary vs. Secondary Sources

In social science, students will be required to cite work and use text-based evidence to support their claims. Students can accomplish this by using primary and secondary sources.

	Examples in the Humanities	Examples in the Sciences
Primary Source	• original, first-hand account of an event or time period • usually written or made during or close to the event or time period • original, creative writing or works of art • factual, not interpretive	• diaries, journals, and letters • government records (census, marriage, military) • photographs, maps, postcards, posters • recorded or transcribed speeches • songs, plays, novels, stories • paintings, drawings, and sculptures
Secondary Source	• analyzes and interprets primary sources • second-hand account of an historical event • interprets creative work	• biographies • histories • literary criticism • book, art, and theater reviews • newspaper articles

Competency 2: Knowledge of time, continuity, and change

1. Identify and analyze historical events that are related by cause and effect.
2. Analyze the sequential nature of historical events using timelines.
3. Analyze examples of primary and secondary source documents for historical perspective.
4. Analyze the impacts of the cultural contributions and technological developments of Africa, the Americas, Asia (including the Middle East), and Europe.
5. Identify the significant historical leaders and events that have influenced Eastern and Western civilizations.
6. Determine the causes and consequences of exploration, settlement, and growth on various cultures.
7. Interpret the ways that individuals and events have influenced economic, social, and political institutions in the world, nation, or state.
8. Analyze immigration and settlement patterns that have shaped the history of the United States.
9. Identify how various cultures contributed to the unique social, cultural, economic, and political features of Florida.
10. Identify the significant contributions of the early and classical civilizations.

History

20th Century Timeline by DECADES

1910 - WWI ends and everyone is happy.
1920 - Lots of expendable income. People living high on the hog. *Great Gatsby* time.
1930 - Crash; no one has money. GREAT DEPRESSION.
1940 - WWII, Japan bombs Pearl Harbor, FDR New Deal, factories.
1945 - atomic bomb, end of WWII.
1945 - Cold War begins when Russia turns USSR (communist).
1951 - **22nd Amendment** limiting presidency to 2 terms of 4 years each.
1957 - Russians launch Sputnik (impacted our scientific exploration).
1960 - US enters Vietnam to combad Communism.
1969 - Moon walk. US wins the Space Race.
1970 - Gasoline crises.
1980 - Reagan and relations with USSR getting better.
1990 - Berlin wall comes down. Cold War ends. USSR becomes Russia again.
1990 - Persian Gulf War (Operation Desert Storm). George **H**. Bush
2000 - Iraq war/war with Afghanistan (Operation Enduring Freedom). George **W**. Bush

> **Quick Tip** - The 20th century is most effectively taught in decades (10 year increments).

World War II

World War II, also know as the Second World War, was a global war that lasted from 1939 to 1945. It involved the vast majority of the world's nations, including all of the great powers. The great powers eventually formed two opposing military alliances: the **Allies** and the **Axis Powers**.

WWII Power Divide

Axis Powers (Bad Guys)	Allied Powers (Good Guys)
Germany (Hitler)	US (Roosevelt)
Italy (Mussolini)	France
Japan (Emperor Hirohito)	Great Britain (Churchill)
	Russia (Stalin)

- At the start of World War II, Russia and Germany were friends. However, Hitler, the leader of Germany, ordered a surprise attack on Russia on June 22, 1941. Russia then became an enemy of the Axis Powers and joined the Allies.
- After Roosevelt died Truman became president.
- Japan bombs Pearl Harbor.
  - This essentially dragged us into WWII.
- Truman Drops drops the atomic bomb on Japan.

Cold War (1947 - 1991)
The Cold War was a state of political and military tension after World War II between powers in the Western Bloc (the United States, its NATO) and powers in the Eastern Bloc (the Soviet Union and its satellite states). The Cold War included:

- **The Space Race**
  - Russians launch Sputnik into space in 1957.
  - U.S. amps up its Space program.
  - Kennedy wants to beat Russia to the moon.
  - 1969 - US lands on the moon.

- **The Arms Race**
  - Between Soviets and US - who can get its nuclear program going first?

Quick Tip:

Television hit the scene shortly after the end of WWII. Therefore, after WWII American culture was greatly influenced by television.

Events and People in History

Franklin Delano Roosevelt - FDR

FDR was President of the United States from 1933 to 1945. He was a Democrat, who won a record four presidential elections. He was seen as a central figure in world events during the mid-20th century. He led the United States during a time of worldwide economic depression and total war. The New Deal was his program for relief, recovery and reform. It also involved a great expansion of the role of the federal government in the economy. Things to remember about FDR are:
- New Deal
- Social Security
- President for 4 terms (unprecedented)

John Locke and the Declaration of Independence

John Locke was a 17th century Englishman who redefined the nature of government. Locke was the most important influence that shaped the founding of the United States According to Locke, a ruler gains authority through the consent of the governed. The duty of that government is to protect the natural rights of the people: life, liberty, and property. If the government should fail to protect these rights, its citizens would have the right to overthrow that government. Locke's ideas deeply influenced Thomas Jefferson as he drafted the **Declaration of Independence.**

Benjamin Franklin

Franklin was one of the Founding Fathers of the United States. Franklin was an author, printer, political theorist, politician, freemason, postmaster, scientist, inventor, civic activist, statesman, and diplomat. He was NOT a senator or president

Why was Plymouth Colonized? - Religion

Plymouth Colony, America's first permanent Puritan settlement, was established by English Separatist Puritans in December 1620. The Pilgrims left England to seek religious freedom.

The Potato Famine, also known as the Great Famine of Ireland

Beginning in 1845 and lasting for six years, the **potato famine** killed over a million men, women and children in Ireland and caused another million to flee the country. The potato famine in Ireland resulted in Irish immigrants coming to the US, causing a huge increase in the Irish population in US cities.

Political Cartoon

In this political cartoon, there are three important figures: President Franklin D. Roosevelt, Congress, and Uncle Sam. Each of them assumes a role in the cartoon, with FDR as the doctor, Congress as the caretaker, and Uncle Sam as the patient. Uncle Sam represents a sick America. America is sick because of the Great Depression. FDR is the doctor, who is working with the Legislative Branch to cure Uncle Sam from the Great Depression. FDR gives Uncle Sam many different kinds of **medicine** which are the bottles on the table. They are special interest groups - NRA is the biggest.

At the time, FDR approved and passed legislation to fix America's financial problems. Many people were doubting whether these programs would actually help or make things worst.

Quick Tip:

This political cartoon shows the President (Executive Branch) working with Congress (Legislative Branch) to solve problems in the U.S.

Women in History and Civil Rights

Harriet Beecher Stowe - an American abolitionist who wrote *Uncle Tom's Cabin*. The novel depicts the harsh life African Americans lived under slavery. The book helped fuel the abolitionist movement to end slavery.

Harriet Tubman - an American abolitionist and humanitarian. Tubman escaped slavery and embarked on missions to rescue approximately seventy enslaved families and friends. She did this by using the network of antislavery activists and safe houses known as the Underground Railroad.

Susan B. Anthony - an American social reformer and feminist who played a pivotal role in the women's suffrage movement.

Betsy Ross - was widely accredited with sewing the American flag.

Landmark Civil Rights Court Cases

Plessy vs. Ferguson (1896) - the decision upholding the constitutionality of state laws requiring racial segregation in public facilities under the doctrine of "separate but equal."

Brown vs. Board of Education (1954) - a landmark United States Supreme Court case in which the Court declared state laws establishing separate public schools for black and white students to be unconstitutional. The decision overturned the *Plessy v. Ferguson* decision of 1896.

Ancient Civilizations

Know what civilizations contributed to the world!

- Greeks - democracy
- China - porcelain
- India - spices
- Mesopotamia - irrigation

> **Crazy Historical Fact:**
> Kings wanted their castles by lots of natural barriers like mountains. Natural barriers provide the kings protection from invading armies.

Italian Renaissance **Lorenzo II Magnifico was a** (patron of the *arts*)
The Renaissance was all about the ARTS! **Lorenzo the Magnificent** ruled the Italian city of Florence as a patron of artists, writers, and humanists. During his reign, the city saw a rebirth of the arts and scholarship that is known as the Renaissance.

Seven *Ancient* Wonders of the World

Great Pyramid at Giza, Egypt

Hanging Gardens of Babylon

Statue of Zeus at Olympia Greece

Temple of Artemis at Ephesus

Mausoleum at Halicarnassus

Colossus of Rhodes

Lighthouse at Alexandria, Egypt.

Understanding timelines and centuries

Centuries are every 100 years
- 15th century is1400 - 1499
- 16th century is 1500 - 1599
- 17th century is 1600 - 1699
- 18th century is 1700 - 1799
- 19th century is 1800 - 1899
- 20th century is 1900 - 1999
- 21st century is 2000 - 2099

> **Remember,** we are in the **21st** Century and our year is **2016**. The century we are in is one up from the number in our year. For example, the 20th Century was the 1900s. The 19th Century was the 1800's and so on.

Decades are every 10 years
Example: *"The 1960s was a tumultuous decade."*

An **era** is a long period in history with a particular characteristic or feature.
Example: *"When Ronald Reagan died, it was the end of an era."*

The U.S. and Native Americans

Europeans brought lots of disease to the Americas when they were exploring the new world. That disease killed millions of Native Americans.

The Fort Laramie Treaty of 1851 was signed on September 17 between United States treaty commissioners and representatives of the several Native American Tribes. The government solution was to assign each tribe a defined territory where they were to remain (reservations).

Quick History:

The Europeans brought diseases to the Americas. That's how they conquered the Native Americans.

Quick History:

The Fort Laramie Treaty was later broken by the U.S. government when gold was discovered on the land that was assigned to the Native American tribes. The U.S. seized back the land and pushed Native Americans farther into isolated territories.

Slavery

America

The first African slaves were brought to the North American colony, Jamestown, Virginia in 1619. They were brought to America to aid in the production of crops such as tobacco and cotton. Slavery was practiced throughout the American colonies in the 17th and 18th centuries; thus, African-American slaves helped build the economic foundations of the United States. A nation-wide debate over slavery tore the nation apart in the American Civil War (1861-65). The Union (North) won the Civil War and slavery was abolished.

Caribbean

America was not the only place where slavery happened. Slaves were brought to the Caribbean to work on sugar plantations. Soon the population of African slaves quickly began to outnumber the Europeans. The proportion of slaves ranged from about one third in Cuba to more than ninety percent in many of the islands. Slave rebellions were common; as rebellions became more frequent, European investors lost money. The costs of maintaining slavery grew higher, and eventually slavery was abolished in the Caribbean as well.

Competency 3: Knowledge of people, places, and environment

1. Identify and apply the six essential elements of geography (i.e., the world in spatial terms, places and regions, physical systems, human systems, environment and society, uses of geography), including the specific terms for each element.
2. Analyze and interpret maps and other graphic representations of physical and human systems.
3. Identify and evaluate tools and technologies (e.g., maps, globe, GPS, satellite imagery) used to acquire, process, and report information from a spatial perspective.
4. Interpret statistics that show how places differ in their human and physical characteristics.
5. Analyze ways in which people adapt to an environment through the production and use of clothing, food, and shelter.
6. Determine the ways tools and technological advances affect the environment.
7. Identify and analyze physical, cultural, economic, and political reasons for the movement of people in the world, nation, or state.
8. Evaluate the impact of transportation and communication networks on the economic development in different regions.
9. Compare and contrast major regions of the world, nation, or state.

Geography

Location

International Date Line (IDL) - an imaginary line of navigation on the surface of the Earth that runs from the north pole to the south pole and indicates the change of one calendar day to the next. It passes through the middle of the Pacific Ocean, roughly following the 180° line of longitude but deviates to pass around some territories and island groups. **The International Date Line** makes detours around political boundaries because the date to the east of the line is one day earlier than that to the west of the line.

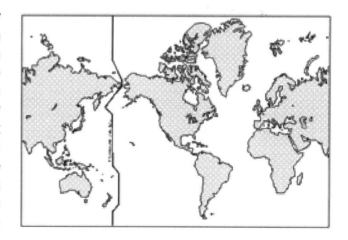

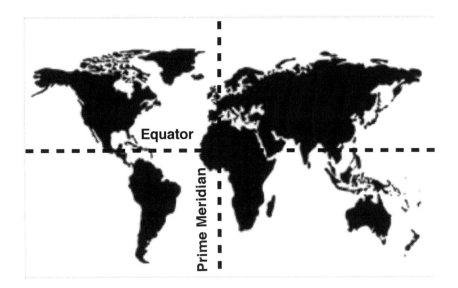

Hemispheres - The prime meridian and the International Date Line create a circle that divides the Earth into the eastern and western hemispheres. This is similar to the way the Equator serves as the 0 latitude line and divides the Earth into the northern and southern hemispheres.

The eastern hemisphere is east of the prime meridian and west of the International Date Line. Most of Earth's landmasses, including all of Asia and Australia, and most of Africa, are part of the eastern hemisphere.

The western hemisphere is west of the prime meridian and east of the International Date Line. The Americas, the western part of the British Isles (including Ireland and Wales), and the northwestern part of Africa are landmasses in the western hemisphere.

Location

The prime meridian, the equator, and the International dateline will give you **absolute location** — the exact spot on the Earth where something is. When describing the absolute location, people use specific coordinates, like latitude and longitude.

Relative location is the location of something in comparison to the **location** of something else.

Scenario
Ms. Jackson is telling students that the Rocky Mountains are west of the Mississippi River. She is giving them the **relative location** of the Rocky Mountains.

Social Science

Maps

Political maps generally show locations of city, towns, and counties, and might have some physical features such as rivers, streams, and lakes. The characteristic of a excellent political map is an simple to use, detailed index. Political maps may be crucial to a researcher's mission to find the counties which include the records of an significant ancestral town.

Physical maps illustrate the physical features of an area, such as the mountains, rivers and lakes. The water is usually shown in blue. Colors are used to show relief— differences in land elevations. Green is typically used at lower elevations, and orange or brown indicate higher elevations.

Road maps show major—some minor highways—and roads, airports, railroad tracks, cities and other points of interest in an area. People use road maps to plan trips and for driving directions.

Special purpose maps are used to help you focus on certain details. Example: topography, climate or district. Special purpose maps can be useful for trying to locate a place, find more about population, for tourism, for elevation, and etc.

- **Climate maps (special purpose)** give general information about the climate and precipitation (rain and snow) of a region. Cartographers, or mapmakers, use colors to show different climate or precipitation zones.

- **Economic or resource maps (special purpose)** feature the type of natural resources or economic activity that dominates an area. Cartographers use symbols to show the locations of natural resources or economic activities. For example, oranges on a map of Florida tell you that oranges are grown there.

- **Topographical Maps (special purpose)** include streams, valleys, rivers, mountains, hills, and more. They also display important landmarks and roads. Topographical maps can often indicate how people migrated and settled the land. They can also provide information about ancestral properties, buildings, local cemeteries, and other important buildings and features.

- **Population Density Maps (special purpose)** measure population per unit area or unit volume. They are frequently applied to living organisms, and most of the time to humans.

Using Charts and Data in Social Science

Population Density
Which country has the highest population density?
Which country has the lowest population density?

Place	Population	Square miles
Cuba	11,382,820	42,803 square miles
India	24,000,265	12,089 square miles
Brazil	24,000,000	67,345 square miles
Ghana	18,409,572	88,811 square miles

Remember, population density is the number of people in relation to the square miles. Be careful. In this example, Ecuador has the highest population density because it has the highest people per square mile. Cuba has the lowest population density because it has the fewest people per square mile.

Net Elevation
Which mountain has the highest NET elevation?
Which mountain is the lowest NET elevation?

Mountain	Sea Level	Elevation
Rainier	Above 300 ft	42,703 ft
Everest	Above 1200 ft	12,089 ft
Kilimanjaro	Below 300 ft	45,000 ft
Rushmore	Below 500 ft	22,800 ft

Remember, you have to factor in the sea-level. Be sure to subtract it from the overall elevation. That gives you the NET elevation. Be careful. In this example, Kilimanjaro looks like the highest. But when you factor in the negative sea level, Rainier beats out Kilimanjaro as having the highest elevation.

Competency 4: Knowledge of government and the citizen

1. Distinguish between the structure, functions, and purposes of federal, state, and local government.
2. Compare and contrast the rights and responsibilities of a citizen in the world, nation, state, and community.
3. Identify and interpret major concepts of the U.S. Constitution and other historical documents.
4. Compare and contrast the ways the legislative, executive, and judicial branches share powers and responsibility.
5. Analyze the U.S. electoral system and the election process.
6. Identify and analyze the relationships between social, economic, and political rights and the historical documents that secure these rights in the United States.
7. Identify and analyze the processes of the U.S. legal system.

Government

Difference between all these crazy historical documents!			
Declaration of Independence	Our break from the Brits.	You don't own me! I have liberty!	Government is no more powerful than man. If Government is tyrannical, people have the right to rebel and start over.
Federalist Papers	We need a government! What would that look like?	85 essays outlining the case for the constitution.	Made the case for checks and balances and separation of powers.
Constitution	This is what our government will look like.	Specific powers granted to the feds.	Articles 1-3 outlined: 1. Legislative, 2. Executive Branch, 3. Judicial Branch (in that order!)

Three Branches of Government
1. Executive - President
2. Legislative - Congress (Senate and House of Representatives
3. Judicial - The courts (Supreme Court)

There is a balance of power among the three branches. No one branch is more powerful than another.

Articles of the Constitution
I. Legislative Branch
II. Executive Branch/Electoral College
III. Judicial Branch
IV. States, Citizenship, New States
V. Amendment Process
VI. Debts, Supremacy, Oaths, Religious Tests
VII. Ratification

Types of Governments:

Dictatorship (Iraq)	Democracy (India)	Theocracy (Iran)	Monarchy (Jordan)
Rule by a single leader who has not been elected but rather who acquired power through violence or force.	In a democracy, the government is elected by the people. All who are eligible to vote — which is a majority of the population — has a chance to have their say over who runs the country.	A form of government where the rulers claim to be ruling based on religious beliefs and ideals. Also, leaders believe they are ruling by the word of god.	A monarchy has a king or queen, who often has absolute power. Power is passed along through the family.
Parliamentary (Israel)	**Republic (USA)**	**Anarchy (Afghanistan?)**	**Oligarchy/Plutocracy (Pakistan)**
A parliamentary system is led by representatives of the people. Each is chosen as a member of a political party and remains in power as long as his/her party does.	A republic is led by representatives of the voters. Each is individually chosen for a set period of time.	Anarchy is a situation where there is no government. This can happen after a civil war in a country.	A form of government which consists of rule by an elite group who rules in its own interests, especially when it comes to the economy and lifestyle.

Quick Tip:
If someone wanted to understand the debate regarding gun control, he or she should consult the Constitution and evaluate whether the right to bear arms includes our right to own an assault riffle.

Bill of Rights:
First 10 Amendments in the Constitution. The first 5 amendments are extremely important to know:
1- The right to speech/press/assembly
2 - The right to bear arms.
3 - You do not have to house a soldier during war.
4 - The police need probable cause to a car, hotel room, house, office.
5 - You don't have to incriminate yourself.

Scenario: A search warrant (4th Amendment) is needed in order for law enforcement to search a hotel room, house, office or other private domain. A search warrant is NOT needed when searching public property like a school locker, or anything within eyeshot.

Courts

Trial Courts - District Courts
Appellate Courts - US Court of Appeals
Supreme Court - The highest court in the U.S. (established in 1789)

> **Quick Tip:**
>
> The Supreme Court settles disputes between States and Feds.

What can states do if legislators cannot agree on a policy and they would like the voters to vote on it in the next election on their ballots? They can use a **Referendum** — the submission of a law to the direct vote of the people. An **example** of a **referendum** is having citizens vote on suggested town curfew laws.

Citizenship

Rights	Responsibilities
Freedom to express yourself.	Support and defend the Constitution.
Freedom to worship as you wish.	Stay informed of the issues affecting your community.
Right to a prompt, fair trial by jury.	Participate in the democratic process.
Right to vote in elections for public officials.	Respect and obey federal, state, and local laws.
Right to apply for federal employment requiring U.S. citizenship.	Respect the rights, beliefs, and opinions of others.
Right to run for elected office.	Participate in your local community.
Freedom to pursue "life, liberty, and the pursuit of happiness."	Pay income and other taxes honestly, and on time, to federal, state, and local authorities.
	Serve on a jury when called upon.
	Defend the country if the need should arise.

(United States Citizen and Immigration Services, 2016)

Elections

When Americans vote for their president, they go to the polls and vote. However, the tally of those votes—the popular vote—does not determine the winner. Instead, Presidential elections use the **Electoral College**. To win the election, a candidate must receive a majority of electoral votes. In the event no candidate receives the majority, the House of Representatives chooses the President and the Senate chooses the Vice President.

Why the Electoral College?
The Electoral College serves as a compromise between election of the President by a vote in Congress and election of the President by a popular vote of qualified citizens.

Each state's number of electors is equal to the number of its U.S. Senators plus the number of its U.S. Representatives. Washington D.C. is given a number of electors equal to the number held by the smallest state. View the division of electors on a map of the U.S (National Archives and Administration, 2016).

Number of Electors
There are a total of 538 electors. A candidate needs the vote of more than half (270) to win the Presidential election.

Quick Tip:

As Alexander Hamilton wrote in *The Federalist Papers*, the Constitution is designed to ensure "that the office of President will never fall to the lot of any man who is not in an eminent degree endowed with the requisite qualifications." Therefore the reason for the Electoral College is to preserve "the sense of the people," while also ensuring the president is chosen "by men most capable of analyzing the qualities adapted to the station, and acting under circumstances favorable to deliberation, and to a judicious combination of all the reasons and inducements which were proper to govern their choice."

Requirements for the Presidency
The U.S. Constitution requires presidential candidates to be:
1. a natural-born citizen of the United States.
2. at least 35 years old.
3. a resident of the United States for 14 years.

Competency 5: Knowledge of production, distribution, and consumption

1. Determine ways that scarcity affects the choices made by governments and individuals.
2. Compare and contrast the characteristics and importance of currency.
3. Identify and analyze the role of markets from production through distribution to consumption.
4. Identify and analyze factors to consider when making consumer decisions.
5. Analyze the economic interdependence between nations (e.g., trade, finance, movement of labor).
6. Identify human, natural, and capital resources and evaluate how these resources are used in the production of goods and services.

Economic Systems

Traditional Economic System - the original economic system in which traditions, customs, and beliefs shape the goods and the services the economy produces.

Command Economic System - the government determines what goods should be produced, how much should be produced and the price at which the goods are offered for sale. Also referred to as Communism.

- **Centralized Control:** A feature of a command economy is that a large part of the economic system is controlled by a centralized power — most often the federal government.

Market Economic System - decisions regarding investment, production, and distribution are based on market, supply and demand. Prices of goods and services are determined in a free price system.

Capitalism and Socialism - formal economies that differ based on the role of the government and equality of economics. Capitalism affords economic freedom, consumer choice, and economic growth.

Mixed Economic System - features characteristics of both capitalism and socialism.

Economic Recession	Economic Depression
Very slow economic growth	Declining business activities
Failure to raise interest rates when needed	Falling prices
High interest rates	Rising unemployment
Overspending	Increasing inventories
Large losses in the business sector	Public fear
	Panic

Monopoly

A monopoly is when a single company or group owns all or nearly all of the market for a type of product or service. A monopoly is characterized by an absence of competition, which often results in high prices and inferior products.

An **assembly line** is a manufacturing process (most of the time called a progressive assembly) in which parts (usually interchangeable parts) are added as the semi-finished assembly moves down the line from workstation to workstation where the parts are added in order by individuals until the final product is assembled. By mechanically moving the parts down an assembly line, a finished product can be assembled faster and with less labor than by having workers carry parts to a stationary piece for assembly.

Immigration

Push-Pull Factors

When people migrate to another country, it is usually because something pushes them away from their native country and pulls them toward a new place. This idea is called the push-pull factor.

Push factors are the circumstances that make a person want to leave. For example, lack of employment or education opportunities, a tyrannical government, famine or war are called push factors.

Quick Tip:

A **PUSH** factor on an Irish family leaving Ireland during the Potato Famine would be the lack of food in the old country. A **PULL** would be food and opportunity to buy more food in another, more prosperous country.

Pull factors are the advantages a country has that make a person want to live there. America has huge pull factors for many people around the world who live with unstable governments, few job opportunities, and no reliable security.

Investing

Opportunity Cost - the loss of potential gain from other alternatives when one alternative is chosen.
- If you buy a video game now, you can't have a bike later. The opportunity is the video game, but the cost is losing the opportunity to buy the bike later.

Investments - higher returns have higher percentages of returns.
7% return is better than a 3% return

Practice Test

1. Florida, Georgia, Mississippi, and Alabama linked together is an example of a:
    E. state.
    F. country.
    G. region.
    H. continent.

2. A map that shows state lines and boundaries is called a:
    A. political map.
    B. special map.
    C. physical map.
    D. typographic map.

3. The United States and China have a:
    A. traditional economy.
    B. command economy.
    C. mixed economy.
    D. market economy.

4. The US Capitol is located about 23 miles north of Alexandria, VA is an example of what type of location?
    A. approximate
    B. absolute
    C. relative
    D. exact

5. Using longitudinal and latitudinal lines along with minutes and seconds will give you what type of location?
    A. relative
    B. absolute
    C. approximate
    D. exact

6. The distance on the Earth's surface for each one degree of latitude or longitude is just over:
    A. 100 miles.
    B. 69 miles.
    C. 4 miles.
    D. 10 miles.

7. _____ are appointed by the president.
    A. Supreme court justices
    B. Congressmen and congresswomen
    C. Senators
    D. Governors

8. This person was a political activist who helped gain women the right to vote.

    A. Betsy Ross

    B. Harriet Tubman

    C. Harriet Beecher Stowe

    D. Susan B. Anthony

9. This person wrote Uncle Tom's Cabin.

    A. Betsy Ross

    B. Harriet Tubman

    C. Harriet Beecher Stowe

    D. Susan B Anthony

10. The above cartoon is this an example of:

    A. Executive Branch and Legislative Branch working together to solve problems.

    B. Executive Branch and the Judicial Branch working together to solve problems.

    C. Executive Branch and Judicial Branch working against each other.

    D. Executive Branch and Legislative Branch working against each other.

11. The most influential person in regards to the United States Constitution and life, liberty, and property is:

    A. John Hobbes.

    B. Andrew Jackson.

    C. John Locke.

    D. George Washington.

12. The Bill of Rights is included in:

    A. Amendments 1-10.

    B. Amendments 1-5.

    C. Amendments 1-6.

    D. Amendments 1-3.

13. Benjamin Franklin was all of these:

    A. Legislator, postmaster, scientists, activist and diplomat.

    B. Senator, politician, postmaster, scientists, activist and diplomat.

    C. President, postmaster, scientists, activist and diplomat.

    D. Inventor, surveyor, politician, postmaster, scientist, activist and diplomat.

14. Plymouth was colonized because colonists were seeking:

    A. political freedom.

    B. religious freedom.

    C. freedom from taxation.

    D. freedom from illegal search and seizure

15. All of the following are rights of a US citizen EXCEPT:

    A. right to vote in elections

    B. right to a speedy trial by jury

    C. right to run for elected office

    D. right to Social Security

16. All of the following are responsibilities of U.S. citizens EXCEPT:

    A. support and defend the constitution.

    B. engage in public service.

    C. stay informed on issues affecting your community.

    D. respect the rights, beliefs and opinions of others.

17. *Uncle Tom's Cabin* is a novel that would mainly appeal to:
    A. abolitionists.
    B. constitutionalists.
    C. academics.
    D. revolutionaries.

18. The Amendment that addresses unlawful search and seizure is Amendment

    _____.

    A. I
    B. II
    C. III
    D. IV

19. The Amendment that gives US citizens the right to peacefully assemble is
    Amendment _____.
    A. I
    B. II
    C. III
    D. IV

20. If a teacher wanted to teach her class about the Civil Rights Movement, which
    would be the best primary source to use?
    A. an interview where someone, who marched on Washington, recounts that day
    B. a textbook outlining the 1960's
    C. Martin Luther King's *I Have a Dream* Speech
    D. music from that time period outlining political protests

21. In Iran, the government rules based on Islamic doctrine. This type of government is
    called a:
    A. theocracy.
    B. monarch.
    C. democracy.
    D. oligarchy.

22. In the U.S. legal system, the person who represents the state government in the
    prosecution of criminal offenses is the:
    A. Public Defender.
    B. District Attorney.
    C. Supreme Court.
    D. Criminal Defense.

23. Congress is part of the _____ branch of government.
    A. Legislative
    B. Executive
    C. Judicial
    D. All of the above

24. Bringing slaves from Africa to the Caribbean resulted in:
    A. cultural innovation.
    B. cultural diffusion.
    C. increased trade between Africa and America.
    D. decreased trade between Africa and America.

25. What would be the best way to help third grade students understand the attributes of the Virginia Colony and persuade people to move to the Virginia Colony?
    A. Draw a poster outlining all the amenities and characteristics Virginia has to offer settlers.
    B. Write a persuasive essay on why Virginia is the best colony in the US.
    C. Research the Virginia Colony in an online encyclopedia.
    D. Bring in a guest speaker to talk about the Virginia Colony back in colonial times.

26. The governments have the right to take private property for public good (i.e. building an interstate through a neighborhood thereby taking private property in the process) is called:
    A. land acquisition.
    B. land accumulation.
    C. imminent domain.
    D. eminent domain.

27. An official ban on trade or other commercial activity with a particular country is called a(n):
    A. boycott.
    B. litigation.
    C. veto.
    D. embargo.

28. What are the Seven Wonders of the Ancient World?
    A. Great Pyramid at Giza, Egypt, Hanging Gardens of Babylon, Statue of Zeus at Olympia, Greece, Temple of Artemis at Ephesus, Mausoleum at Halicarnassus, Colossus of Rhodes, Eiffel Tower
    B. Great Pyramid at Giza, Egypt, Hanging Gardens of Babylon, Statue of Zeus at Olympia, Greece, Temple of Artemis at Ephesus, Mausoleum at Halicarnassus, Colossus of Rhodes, Lighthouse at Alexandria, Egypt
    C. Grand Canyon, Hanging Gardens of Babylon, Statue of Zeus at Olympia, Greece, Temple of Artemis at Ephesus, Mausoleum at Halicarnassus, Colossus of Rhodes, Lighthouse at Alexandria, Egypt
    D. Great Pyramid at Giza, Niagara Falls, Statue of Zeus at Olympia, Greece, Temple of Artemis at Ephesus, Mausoleum at Halicarnassus, Colossus of Rhodes, Lighthouse at Alexandria, Egypt

29. The Treaty of Fort Laramie in 1868 granted the Sioux nation ownership of the Black Hills, which were considered sacred grounds for the Sioux. That treaty was broken when:
    A. The United States Government seized the land when gold was found there.
    B. General Custer went on the Black Hills Expedition to choose a location for a new Army fort and to investigate the area's natural resources.
    C. the Sioux moved across the country to California.
    D. the Sioux waged war of General Custer before he got to Black Hills.

30. Why were Europeans able to conquer so many Native Americans?
    A. Europeans had more people with them than the Native Americans did.
    B. The Native Americans did not know who to fight in a sophisticated war.
    C. Europeans brought diseases with them to the U.S., which weakened the Native Americans.
    D. Europeans had weapons, and the Native Americans did not.

31. The best way to teach students the United States time zones is by using:
    A. a flat map with the lines of the time zones clearly identified.
    B. a TV broadcast from another time zone.
    C. a globe with a fixed light source shining on it.
    D. a flat world map with visible longitude and latitude lines.

32. The Cold War was a state of political and military tension between:
    A. U.S. and Germany.
    B. U.S. and Russia.
    C. U.S. and Iraq.
    D. U.S. and Afghanistan.

33. What Article of the Constitution established the Legislative Branch of the United States of America?
    A. Article I
    B. Article II
    C. Article III
    D. Article IV

34. What Article of the Constitution includes the electoral college?
    A. Article I
    B. Article II
    C. Article III
    D. Article IV

35. Why was the electoral college included in the U.S. Constitution?
    A. to equalize voting power in states that had smaller populations than other states
    B. to give the electoral college ultimate power over the election process
    C. to help voters make informed decisions in electing the highest officials
    D. both A and C

36. When a map's features show a real object with accurate sizes reduced or enlarged by a certain amount, the map is said to be:
    A. scale.
    B. key.
    C. representative.
    D. accurate.

37. A _____ is prolonged period of high inflation, high unemployment and increased public fear.
    A. depression
    B. stagnation
    C. recession
    D. inflation

38. Who conducts impeachment trials in the U.S.?

   A. The Supreme Court

   B. The House of representatives

   C. The Senate

   D. The President

39. In a market economy, competition is supposed to:

   A. drive prices down.

   B. drive prices up.

   C. keep prices the same.

   D. fluctuate prices.

40. The _____ is a line that runs between Russia and Alaska and goes around political boundaries in the Pacific ocean.

   A. Prime Meridian

   B. International Dateline

   C. equator

   D. latitude and longitude

41. What would be the best way to teach third grade students about the Battle of Bunker Hill?

   A. Write a persuasive essay explaining their positions about the Battle of Bunker Hill.

   B. Have students read the chapter in the textbook on the Battle of Bunker Hill.

   C. Look at a map to determine where the Battle of Bunker Hill took place.

   D. Use cooperative learning groups to research the battle and then role play what they have discovered.

42. If a teacher wants to have an open conversation with a student who has trouble communicating with the teacher, the teacher might try:

   A. a double entry journal.

   B. a dialogue journal.

   C. a letter home to the student's parents.

   D. sending the student to the guidance counselor.

43. Mr. Lopez wants to explain how awesome the Seven Ancient Wonders of the World are. What would be the best way to engage students?

    A. Have a guest speaker come in and talk about the Seven Ancient Wonders of the World.

    B. Look at a map to discover where the Seven Ancient Wonders of the World are.

    C. Read about the Seven Ancient Wonders of the World in a text book.

    D. Take a virtual tour on the internet of the Seven Ancient Wonders of the World.

44. The End of Course (EOC) Exam given to every student in the state to determine proficiency is considered a:

    A. criterion-referenced assessment.

    B. norm-reference assessment.

    C. formative assessment.

    D. informal assessment.

45. Which of the following do state governments have the authority to do?

    A. regulate foreign commerce

    B. regulate trade

    C. oversee national defense

    D. establish a postal service

46. The states considered part of the Sunbelt are:

    A. Washington, Massachusetts, New York.

    B. Florida, Texas, California.

    C. Georgia, Louisiana, Alabama.

    D. North Dakota, South Dakota, Colorado.

47. The draining of the Florida Everglades was due to:

    A. population increase.

    B. war with Native Americans.

    C. trade.

    D. agriculture.

48. Who designed and carried out the Boston Tea Party?

    A. Samuel Adams

    B. Paul Riviere

    C. George Washington

    D. Patrick Henry

49. Who wrote the Federalist Papers?

    A. Alexander Hamilton, James Madison, and Ben Franklin

    B. Alexander Hamilton, James Madison, and John Jay

    C. John Locke, James Madison, and John Jay

    D. Alexander Hamilton, Andrew Jackson, and Ben Franklin

50. Which country was NOT part of the Axis Powers during WWII?

    A. Germany

    B. Japan

    C. France

    D. Italy

Answers - Social Science Practice Test

1. C	16. B	31. C	46. B
2. A	17. A	32. B	47. D
3. C	18. D	33. A	48. A
4. C	19. A	34. B	49. B
5. B	20. C	35. D	50. C
6. B	21. A	36. A	
7. A	22. B	37. A	
8. D	23. A	38. C	
9. C	24. B	39. A	
10. A	25. A	40. B	
11. C	26. D	41. D	
12. A	27. D	42. B	
13. D	28. B	43. D	
14. B	29. A	44. A	
15. D	30. C	45. B	

Answer Explanations - Social Science

1. **C**. Regions are areas, large and small, that share common features: language, government, religion, forests, wildlife, and climate. A region is a basic unit of geography. The three states, Florida, Georgia, Mississippi are part of a region.
2. **A**. Political maps show governmental boundaries of countries, states, counties, and major cities.
3. **C**. A mixed economic system combines private and public enterprise. China and the U.S. have both private and public enterprises.
4. **C**. Relative location is when something is compared to the location of something else.
5. **B**. Absolute location is the location of a place based on a fixed point on Earth using latitude and longitude coordinates.
6. **B**. Each degree of latitude is approximately 69 miles (111 kilometers) apart.
7. **A**. Congress people, senators and governors are all elected by the people. Only Supreme Court Justices are appointed.
8. **D**. Susan B. Anthony was an American social reformer and women's rights activist. She played a pivotal role in the women's suffrage movement.
9. **C**. Harriet Beecher Stowe was an American abolitionist and author, who wrote *Uncle Tom's Cabin*. *Uncle Tom's Cabin* shed light on the horrible conditions of slavery and racism.
10. **A**. In this cartoon, FDR is the president (the executive branch), and he is leaning over talking to Congress (the legislative branch). Together they are trying to fix a sick Uncle Sam (the United States). This cartoon was taken from the New Deal era, when FDR was trying to pull the U.S. out of the depression.
11. **C**. Commonly known as the "father of liberalism," John Locke was a philosopher and physician. He was widely regarded as one of the most influential of Enlightenment thinkers. Locke's philosophy on liberty and the social contract influenced the written works of Alexander Hamilton, James Madison, Thomas Jefferson, and other Founding Fathers of the United States.
12. **A**. The first ten amendments to the US Constitution are the Bill of Rights. They were ratified in 1791 and guarantee rights such as the freedoms of speech, assembly, and worship.
13. **D**. Ben Franklin was a lot of things, but he was neither a president nor a representative.
14. **B**. The Pilgrims left England to colonize Plymouth to seek religious freedom and find a better life.

15. **D**. The table below shows the rights and responsibilities of U.S. citizens.
16. **B**. The table below shows the rights and responsibilities of U.S. citizens.

Rights	Responsibilities
Freedom to express yourself.	Support and defend the Constitution.
Freedom to worship as you wish.	Stay informed of the issues affecting your community.
Right to a prompt, fair trial by jury.	Participate in the democratic process.
Right to vote in elections for public officials.	Respect and obey federal, state, and local laws.
Right to apply for federal employment requiring U.S. citizenship.	Respect the rights, beliefs, and opinions of others.
Right to run for elected office.	Participate in your local community.
Freedom to pursue "life, liberty, and the pursuit of happiness."	Pay income and other taxes honestly, and on time, to federal, state, and local authorities.
	Serve on a jury when called upon.
	Defend the country if the need should arise.

17. **A**. *Uncle Tom's Cabin* is a story about the atrocities of slavery. It is a book that fueled the abolitionist movement (the movement to end slavery).
18. **D**. The Fourth Amendment of the U.S. Constitution provides, "[t]he right of the people to be secure in their persons, houses, papers, and effects, against unreasonable searches and seizures, shall not be violated…"
19. **A**. The First Amendment (Amendment I) to the United States Constitution prohibits the making of any law respecting an establishment of religion, impeding the free exercise of religion, abridging the freedom of speech, infringing on the freedom of the press, interfering with the right to peaceably assemble, or prohibiting the petitioning for a governmental redress of grievances.
20. **C**. A primary source is an original source or evidence. Martin Luther King's speech is an original document.
21. **A**. A theocracy is a system of government in which priests rule in the name of God or a god.
22. **B**. In the U.S., a District Attorney (DA) represents a state government in the prosecution of criminal offenses. The DA is also the chief law enforcement officer and legal officer of that state's jurisdiction.
23. **A**. The legislative branch is made up of the two houses of Congress—the Senate and the House of Representatives. It is the duty of the legislative branch is to make laws.
24. **B**. Cultural diffusion is when cultural beliefs and social activities are spread through different ethnicities, religions, and nationalities. During the slave trade, goods, services, identities and cultural were diffused across continents.
25. **A**. In this example, drawing a poster would be the best way to showcase attributes of the colony. A marketing poster fits this better than role play because role play requires players and a situation to act out. A persuasive essay is not as effective as a marketing poster. A guest speaker would be least effective.
26. **D**. Eminent domain is the authority of a government or its agent to expropriate private property for public use.

27. **D**. An embargo is when one country refuses to do business with another country. A boycott is when private citizens refuse to buy products from a company. Litigation is the process of taking legal action. A veto is a constitutional right to reject a decision or proposal made by a law-making body.

28. **B**. Niagara Falls, The Grand Canyon, and The Eiffel Tower are not part of the Ancient wonders of the world.

29. **A**. The treaty gave the Black Hills to the Native Americans and was to be henceforth closed to all whites. However, workers seeking gold had crossed the reservation borders, in violation of the treaty. Indians had assaulted these gold prospectors, in violation of the treaty, and war ensued. The U.S. government seized the Black Hills land in 1877.

30. **C**. The diseases brought to the U.S. by the Europeans included bubonic plague, chicken pox, pneumonic plague, cholera, diphtheria, influenza, measles, scarlet fever, smallpox, typhus, tuberculosis, and whooping cough.

31. **C**. A globe with a fixed light source shows when the Sun shines on one side of the Earth, the other side of the Earth is dark. This can simulate different times of day as the globe turns toward the light source.

32. **B**. Although the the term "cold" is used because there was no large-scale fighting directly between the two sides, the U.S. and Russia, the Cold War was very contentious, and both sides feared a nuclear invasion.

33. **A**. Article I says, "All legislative Powers herein granted shall be vested in a Congress of the United States, which shall consist of a Senate and House of Representatives."

34. **B**. "Each State shall appoint, in such Manner as the Legislature thereof may direct, a Number of Electors, equal to the whole Number of Senators and Representatives to which the State may be entitled in the Congress: but no Senator or Representative, or Person holding an Office of Trust or Profit under the United States, shall be appointed an Elector." (U.S. Const. amend. II).

35. **D**. The Electoral College was created to buffer between population and the selection of a President (The founding fathers didn't trust the people to make a sound decision in electing a president). It was also created as part of the structure of the government that gave extra power to the smaller states. Without the electoral college, big states with more population would have more power in electing a president.

36. **A**. Map drawn to scale refers to the relationship (or ratio) between distance on a map and the corresponding distance on the ground. For example, on a **1:100000** scale map, **1cm** on the map equals 1km on the ground. The map is proportional to the real distance on the ground.

37. **A**. A depression is a severe and prolonged downturn in economic activity.

Economic Recession	Economic Depression
Very slow economic growth	Declining business activities
Failure to raise interest rates when needed	Falling prices
High interest rates	Rising unemployment
Overspending	Increasing inventories
Large losses in the business sector	Public fear
	Panic

38. **C.** The Constitution requires a two-thirds vote of the Senate to convict, and the penalty for an impeached official is removal from office.

39. **A.** Competition among a bunch of different people for one product drives the price in a market down. Competition can even cause the price to move as low as the supply price and forces vendors to supply the most wanted products at the lowest resource cost.

40. **B.** The International Date Line separates two consecutive calendar dates.

41. **D.** In this example, role play would be the best choice because there is a situation (the battle) and characters (generals, and soldiers on different sides).

42. **B.** Dialogue journals allow students to write down their feelings and observations without having to same them out loud. Some students can write how they feel better than they can verbalize how they feel. It's called a dialogue journal because it facilitates a conversation.

43. **D.** A virtual tour would be a way for students to see the Seven Ancient Wonders of the World without having to actually go there. The other choices are not as effective as a virtual tour.

44. **A.** A criterion-referenced test measures student performance against a fixed set of predetermined **criteria, or learning standards**. The End of Course exams (EOCs) measure student performance on the Florida Standards.

45. **B.** The U.S. Constitution allows states to regulate trade that occurs within the state borders. The other 3 choices in this item (post office, foreign commerce, national defense) are part of the federal government's domain.

46. **B.** The Sunbelt is the region in the U.S. that stretches across the southern and southwestern portions of the country from Florida to California.

47. **D.** Early Florida settlers wanted drained the 4,000 square miles of Everglades, in south Florida to create farmland. They did this by digging canals that would draw off the swamp water and allow it to flow to the ocean.

48. **A.** Samuel Adams was one of Boston's prominent revolutionary leaders. He was able to garner large support for the Boston Tea Party.

49. **B.** Alexander Hamilton, James Madison, and John Jay wrote the Federalist Papers — a collection of 85 articles and essays promoting the ratification of the Constitution.

50. **C.** Axis Powers included Japan, Germany and Italy.

Additional Practice - Social Science

An important skill in slaying the test, is the ability to transfer knowledge from one area to another. That way, no matter how the questions are worded, you have the transfer skills and the flexible thinking to answer accurately. We find that writing your own items for each sub-skill on the test is a great way to sharpen your transfer skills. When you write your own test questions while studying, you're thinking like a test maker and not a test taker!

The following pages provide you an opportunity to write your own test questions for each competency and its sub-skills.

Competency 1: Knowledge of effective instructional practices and assessment

sub-skill	test question	answer choices
Select appropriate resources for instructional delivery of social science concepts, including complex informational text.		
Identify appropriate resources for planning for instruction of social science concepts.		
Choose appropriate methods for assessing social science concepts.		
Determine appropriate learning environments for social science lessons.		

Competency 2: Knowledge of time, continuity, and change

sub-skill	test question	answer choices
Identify and analyze historical events that are related by cause and effect.		
Analyze the sequential nature of historical events using timelines.		
Analyze examples of primary and secondary source documents for historical perspective.		
Analyze the impacts of the cultural contributions and technological developments of Africa, the Americas, Asia (including the Middle East), and Europe.		
Identify the significant historical leaders and events that have influenced Eastern and Western civilizations.		
Determine the causes and consequences of exploration, settlement, and growth on various cultures.		
Interpret the ways that individuals and events have influenced economic, social, and political institutions in the world, nation, or state.		
Analyze immigration and settlement patterns that have shaped the history of the United States.		
Identify how various cultures contributed to the unique social, cultural, economic, and political features of Florida.		
Identify the significant contributions of the early and classical civilizations.		

Competency 3: Knowledge of people, places, and environment

sub-skill	test question	answer choices
Identify and apply the six essential elements of geography (i.e., the world in spatial terms, places and regions, physical systems, human systems, environment and society, uses of geography), including the specific terms for each element.		
Analyze and interpret maps and other graphic representations of physical and human systems.		
Identify and evaluate tools and technologies (e.g., maps, globe, GPS, satellite imagery) used to acquire, process, and report information from a spatial perspective.		
Interpret statistics that show how places differ in their human and physical characteristics.		
Analyze ways in which people adapt to an environment through the production and use of clothing, food, and shelter.		
Determine the ways tools and technological advances affect the environment.		
Identify and analyze physical, cultural, economic, and political reasons for the movement of people in the world, nation, or state.		
Evaluate the impact of transportation and communication networks on the economic development in different regions.		
Compare and contrast major regions of the world, nation, or state.		

Competency 4: Knowledge of government and the citizen

sub-skill	test question	answer choices
Distinguish between the structure, functions, and purposes of federal, state, and local government.		
Compare and contrast the rights and responsibilities of a citizen in the world, nation, state, and community.		
Identify and interpret major concepts of the U.S. Constitution and other historical documents.		
Compare and contrast the ways the legislative, executive, and judicial branches share powers and responsibility.		
Analyze the U.S. electoral system and the election process.		
Identify and analyze the relationships between social, economic, and political rights and the historical documents that secure these rights in the United States.		
Identify and analyze the processes of the U.S. legal system.		
Evaluate the impact of transportation and communication networks on the economic development in different regions.		
Compare and contrast major regions of the world, nation, or state.		

This page is intentionally left blank

III. Science

This chapter provides an overview of the competencies for the science section of Elementary ED (K-6) Subject Area Exam. This section has explanations regarding all the competencies tested on the exam as well as in-depth analysis of the types of questions students will encounter when taking this test.

The competencies addressed in this chapter are from the Florida Teacher Certification Examination Test Information Guide.

You can access that using this link:
http://www.fl.nesinc.com/PDFs/ElemEd_K-6_TIG_4thEd_DOE040115.pdf

Competency 1 - Knowledge of effective science instruction

1. Analyze and apply developmentally appropriate researched-based strategies for teaching science practices.
2. Select and apply safe and effective instructional strategies to utilize manipulatives, models, scientific equipment, real-world examples, and print and digital representations to support and enhance science instruction.
3. Identify and analyze strategies for formal and informal learning experiences to provide science curriculum that promotes students' innate curiosity and active inquiry (e.g., hands-on experiences, active engagement in the natural world, student interaction).
4. Select and analyze collaborative strategies to help students explain concepts, to introduce and clarify formal science terms, and to identify misconceptions.
5. Identify and apply appropriate reading strategies, mathematical practices, and science-content materials to enhance science instruction for learners at all levels.
6. Apply differentiated strategies in science instruction and assessments based on student needs.
7. Identify and apply ways to organize and manage a classroom for safe, effective science teaching that reflect state safety procedures and restrictions (e.g., procedures, equipment, disposal of chemicals, classroom layout, use of living organisms).
8. Select and apply appropriate technology, science tools and measurement units for students' use in data collection and the pursuit of science.
9. Select and analyze developmentally appropriate diagnostic, formative and summative assessments to evaluate prior knowledge, guide instruction, and evaluate student achievement.
10. Choose scientifically and professionally responsible content and activities that are socially and culturally sensitive.

Teaching Methods for Science

First things first, science is inquiry based, meaning students must be given the opportunity to interact with the concepts they are studying. For example, talking about living and non-living things is one thing. However, going outside and **_observing_** living and non-living things is quite another. Students have to have the opportunity to touch, observe, and interact with the environment they are studying.

According to the National Science Teacher Association or NSTA (2009), effective science instruction includes:

Scenario

If the teacher wants her students to understand the diet of an owl, she should give them an opportunity to dissect owl pellets (owl poop). Reading about owl diets is ok. But dissecting poop is so much better!

- having pedagogical knowledge.
- providing learning opportunities that meet the individual needs of students, placing the learner at the center of instruction.
- facilitating learning opportunities that develop students' conceptual understanding.

In a nutshell, teachers must know the science content (pedagogy), empower the students to learn, differentiate to meet the needs of diverse population, and foster inquiry based learning activities. Students have to touch, feel and observe to understand science. Textbooks are important, but only using a textbook for science instruction is unacceptable.

Safety

Safety is important when providing students the opportunity to learn in a science classrooms. Teachers must communicate procedures and guidelines repeatedly, so students understand what is expected in terms of safety and security.

Here are some dos and don'ts when it comes to science classroom safety:

> **Remember Developmental Appropriate Practices (DAP):**
>
> Match the students' age to the appropriate task. For example, 4-6 graders might have to interact with chemicals during labs, while K-3 would probably not.

Do	**Don't**
Communicate procedures over and over again and provide lots of practice with students to engage in procedures and emergency operations. Practice makes perfect! Also, send procedures home for parents to read and sign indicating they received the procedures and understood them.	Post procedures on the wall and expect students review them on their own.
Lock up chemicals, sharp tools and other hazardous materials used in labs.	Leave chemicals, sharp tools and other hazardous materials in safe place near your desk.
Leave the chemical safety manual out where students can access it in case there is an emergency with chemicals.	Lock up the chemical manual with the chemicals so only the person with a key can access it.
Predetermine student lab groups to maximize time on task and minimize student misbehavior, accidents, or mishaps.	Let students get into groups on their own before the lab.
Keep your principal and administration informed whenever you are doing a lab or controversial science unit.	Send notes home to let parents know about the labs. If there is a problem, then contact your administration.

ELLs and Science Instruction

Science is a great way to engage with your ELL students. Science, in many ways, transcends language because every student has a sense of wonder and inquiry. A cell, a rock, and a molecule are the same in one language to another.

To maximize ELL participation and mastery of science concepts you can:
- provide ELL students with science materials in their native language.
- use translators or paraprofessionals to help you explain complex science concepts in students' native language.

Be careful! If you give students a writing assignment in science, you are also assessing writing in English. So if teachers want to measure ELL students' understanding of science concepts, a science diagnostic test, *in Spanish,* is the best way to do that. That way the teacher is assessing science skills and not English language skills.

Assessments

Assessments are essential in effective science instruction. Assessments come in all different forms: diagnostic, formative, summative, and authentic.

Diagnostic Assessments:
In science, teachers use diagnostic assessments to identify preconceptions and misconceptions. Teachers give diagnostic assessments in the beginning of the year, semester, quarter or even at the beginning of a unit. The results from diagnostic tests can be used to differentiate instruction based on student needs and as a baseline to measure student learning.

Formative Assessments
Formative assessments in science, as in other areas, are used throughout the learning experience. Formative assessments can consist of observing students in a lab to see if they understand the application of the concepts. Formative assessments can also be an exit slip at the end of a complex science lesson to determine understanding.

Summative Assessments
Summative assessments are used at the end of learning. Typically summative assessments are mid-terms, finals, and state-mandated tests.

Authentic Assessments
Authentic assessments in science are essential in understanding if a student understands how to apply the knowledge to a task. Performance and project based assessments in science are considered authentic assessments. An example performance based or project based assessment is a lab or a presentation where students have to move beyond simply answering multiple choice questions, and use higher order thinking and application skills.

Scenario - A testing cycle in an effective classroom during a unit on rocks would be:
- A **diagnostic** test to determine preconceptions and misconceptions about rocks.
- **Differentiated** instruction based on diagnostic data.
- **Formative** assessments, in the form of observations, exit slips and other formatives throughout the learning.
- **Differentiated** instruction and modifications based the formative assessments.
- A **project/performance-based** assessment in the form of a lab where students form a hypothesis, test their hypothesis have to go through a series of experiments, and write up their results.
- A **summative** assessment at the end of the rock unit.

Technology in Science Class

Technology can enhance the learning environment in science class. Guidelines for using technology differ from district to district and state to state. It is important teachers review their own district's and school's guidelines regarding tech in the classroom.

Virtual Labs
Virtual labs are a great way to engage students. Students can input data, gather information and conduct an experiment in a virtual lab. Virtual labs are also great because they allow students the experience even if funds are not available for the physical lab.

Technology tools
Students use a **data base** to find other studies that relate to their topics. Students use a **spread sheet** to store their data from an experiment. Students would use **presentation software** like PowerPoint or Keynote to present their findings to the class. Teachers must know when and how to use these tools effectively.

Professionally, Socially and Culturally Responsible Science Instruction

Just like in English class, science class should give all students an opportunity to engage in socially and culturally responsive topics. Students should have the opportunity to learn about women in science and the contributions all cultures have made in science.

Bias
Textbooks can be biased. They are written from one perspective. Therefore, it's important teachers draw from an array of material that explains concepts. Teachers should also try to refrain from inserting any bias into science instruction. Remember, textbooks are resources NOT the curriculum.

Controversy
Science is full of controversy, and teachers can often encounter push back when they explore topics like DNA, stem cell research, evolution and more. The best thing a teacher can do is keep her principal or administration informed about any topics that may be controversial. That way when the school gets a call from a concerned parent about a controversial topic, the administration is prepared. When in doubt, tell your principal to cover all your bases.

Scenario

A third grade teacher thinks that the chapter on evolution will spark controversy. What should she do?
   a. Allow students to opt out of the lesson if they prefer not to participate. (**NO**! They key word here is third grade. 3rd graders don't know if they want to opt out or not.)
   b. Tell her principal about the unit. (**YES**! Always keep admin informed.)
   c. Send a letter home, letting parents know about the unit. (**NO**! This may cause a problem where there wasn't one. Let the principal decide if you should bring attention to the unit with an email home. Otherwise, don't do it!)
   d. Teach the lesson and make a decision if a student's parent calls. (**NO**! This is reactive not proactive.)

Competency 2 - Knowledge of the nature of science

1. Analyze the dynamic nature of science models, laws, mechanisms, and theories that explain natural phenomena (e.g., durability, tentativeness, replication, reliance on evidence).
2. Identify and apply science and engineering practices through integrated process skills (e.g., observing, classifying, predicting, hypothesizing, designing and carrying out investigations, developing and using models, constructing and communicating explanations).
3. Differentiate between the characteristics of experiments (e.g., multiple trials, control groups, variables) and other types of scientific investigations (e.g., observations, surveys).
4. Identify and analyze attitudes and dispositions underlying scientific thinking (e.g., curiosity, openness to new ideas, appropriate skepticism, cooperation).
5. Identify and select appropriate tools, including digital technologies, and units of measurement for various science tasks.
6. Evaluate and interpret pictorial representations, charts, tables, and graphs of authentic data from scientific investigations to make predictions, construct explanations, and support conclusions.
7. Identify and analyze ways in which science is an interdisciplinary process and interconnected to STEM disciplines (i.e., science, technology, engineering, mathematics).
8. Analyze the interactions of science and technology with society including cultural, ethical, economic, political, and global factors.

Models, Laws, Mechanisms, & Theories

Scientists use **models** to communicate ideas and to represent abstract phenomena. For example, the Solar System is impossible to see in a classroom or lab; however, a model of the Solar System is easily accessible in a classroom or lab. Scientific **theories** are based on a body of evidence and many experiments, trials and tests. **Theories** are explanations for observable phenomena. Science **theories** are based on a body of evidence developed over time. Scientific **explanations** describe the mechanisms for natural events. Scientific **laws** are regularities or mathematical descriptions of natural phenomena. A **hypothesis** is used by scientists as an idea that may contribute important new knowledge for the evaluation of a scientific theory.

Students in science:

- Observe - employ the 5 senses to interact with phenomena and recording findings.
- Classify - arrange living and non living things based on attributes.
- Predict - make assumptions based on evidence.
- Hypothesize - state a prediction based on evidence.
- Investigate - carry out experiments.

Experiments

An experiment is a procedure carried out to refute or validate a hypothesis. Experiments provide help students understand cause-and-effect relationships by demonstrating what outcome occurs when a particular factor is manipulated.

An experiment usually has three kinds of variables: independent, dependent, and controlled. The independent variable the one that is changed by the scientist.
- Independent variable - the element manipulated in the experiment.
- Dependent variable - the observed changed.
- Control - quantities that a scientist wants to remain constant, and she must observe them as carefully as the dependent variables.

Example:

If a scientists wants to test the effectiveness of a fertilizer, she might make a hypothesis, "Fertilizer A will increase the growth of the plant by 15% over no fertilizer at all."

To test the hypothesis, she would place two plant bulbs of the same plant and same size in two different pots. The pots are the same size. She uses the same amount of water, same amount of light, same everything. Those are the controls. The only thing that is different is the **independent variable**, which is Fertilizer A.

Fertilizer A is added to this plant. It is the **independent variable.**

No fertilizer is added to this pot.

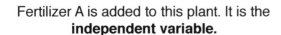

The **dependent** variable is the measured changed because of the Fertilizer. In this example the measured change is the growth of the flowers.

Competency 3 - Knowledge of physical sciences

1. Identify and differentiate among the physical properties of matter (e.g., mass, volume, texture, hardness, freezing point).
2. Identify and differentiate between physical and chemical changes (e.g., tearing, burning, rusting).
3. Compare the properties of matter during phase changes through the addition and/or removal of energy (e.g., boiling, condensation, evaporation).
4. Differentiate between the properties of homogeneous mixtures (i.e., solutions) and heterogeneous mixtures.
5. Identify examples of and relationships among atoms, elements, molecules, and compounds.
6. Identify and compare potential and kinetic energy.
7. Differentiate among forms of energy, transformations of energy, and their real-world applications (e.g., chemical, electrical, mechanical, heat, light, sound).
8. Distinguish among temperature, heat, and forms of heat transfer (e.g., conduction, convection, radiation).
9. Analyze the functionality of an electrical circuit based on its conductors, insulators, and components.
10. Identify and apply the characteristics of contact forces (e.g., push, pull, friction), at-a-distance forces (e.g., magnetic, gravitational, electrostatic), and their effects on matter (e.g., motion, speed).

States of Matter

- **Solid** - particles are very close together.
- **Liquid** - particles are closer together than a gas but farther apart than a solid.
- **Gas** - particles are very far apart.

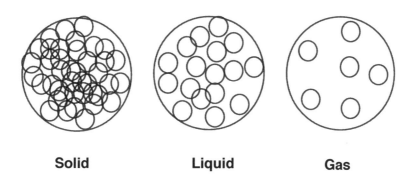

Solid   **Liquid**   **Gas**

Changes in Matter

Physical - results in change in the size and shape by:	Chemical - results in any change that forms new substances at the molecular level by:
tearing	rotting
folding	burning
melting	cooking
freezing	rusting
evaporating	
cutting	

Phase Changes in Matter

Changes in matter can happen by removing or adding energy in the form of boiling, condensation, and evaporation.

Boiling - rapid vaporization of a liquid (liquid to gas).

Condensation - water that collects as droplets on a cold surface when humid air is in contact with it (gas to liquid).

Evaporation - vaporization of a liquid that occurs from the surface of a liquid into a gaseous phase (liquid to gas.

Quick Fact:

Have you ever walked into a grocery store after you worked out, and you are freezing? That's because when water evaporates, it leaves behind cooler air. It's called *temperature moderation*, and it's the amazing property of water a property that is essential for life on Earth.

Renewable Resources vs NonRenewable Resources

renewable	nonrenewable - limited
solar	fossil fuels
wind	coal
hydro power	natural gas
	nuclear energy

Mixtures

A mixture is a material system made up of two or more different substances which are mixed but are not combined chemically. The identity of the mixed elements are retained in a mixture. There are two types of mixtures: h**omogenous** and **heterogenous**.

Homogenous Mixture	Heterogenous Mixture	Collioid	Suspension	Solutions
homo = same	hetero = different	homogenous mixture	heterogeneous mixture	homogeneous mixture
You cannot see different parts of the mixture.	You can see different parts of the mixture.	One substance of microscopically dispersed insoluble particles is suspended throughout another substance. Particles do not settle and cannot be separated out by ordinary filtering.	Contains solid particles that are sufficiently large for sedimentation.	The dissolving agent is the solvent.
coffee, peanut butter, Koolaid	chicken noodle soup, cereal	gels, and emulsions	orange juice, salad dressing,	salt water, sugar water

Atoms, Elements, Molecules, and Compounds

Atoms - the basic unit of a chemical elements. More than 99.94% of an atom's mass is in the nucleus.

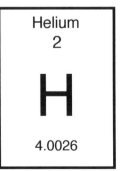

Electrons - negatively charged subatomic particles that circle around the atom's nucleus.
Neutrons - neutrally charged subatomic particles and are located in the nucleus of the atom.
Protons - positively charged subatomic particles and are located in the nucleus.

Elements - more than one hundred substances that cannot be chemically interconverted or broken down into simpler substances and are primary constituents of matter.

Atomic Number - how an element is identified. It is also the number of protons in the nuclei of its atoms.

| Helium |
| 2 |
| **H** |
| 4.0026 |

Molecules - the smallest particle in a chemical element or compound that has the chemical properties of that element or compound. **Molecules** are made up of atoms that are held together by chemical bonds.

H₂O

Water is the molecule H_2O (2 hydrogen elements and 1 oxygen element). Together the elements in this molecule make up the amazing water molecule.

Compounds are composed of two or more elements bonded together. All compounds are molecules, but not all molecules are compounds.

Notice:

Molecules *can* be made up of multiples of a single element like oxygen (O2), while compounds *must* be made up of two different molecules (CO2).

Compounds/ Molecules	Only Molecules
CO2	O2
H2O	H2
CH4	N2

Ions are a charged element or molecule that have lost or gained 1 or more electrons.

Isotopes are two or more forms of the same element that have the same number of protons but a different number of neutrons.

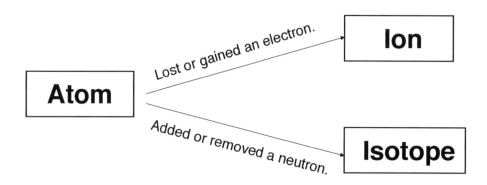

Energy

Energy is a property that can be transferred in between and among objects. Energy can also by converted into different forms.

Kinetic Energy - object is in motion. It is the actually moving of an object. For example, a rock rolling down a hill or a swing swinging in the air both have kinetic energy. Because the objects are IN MOTION, they have kinetic energy.

Potential Energy - the energy possessed by an object or individual by virtue of its position relative to others, stresses within itself, electric charge, and other factors. For example, a rock on the top of the hill, before is rolls down, has potential energy. It has the potential to roll down.

Potential - at the top of the hill

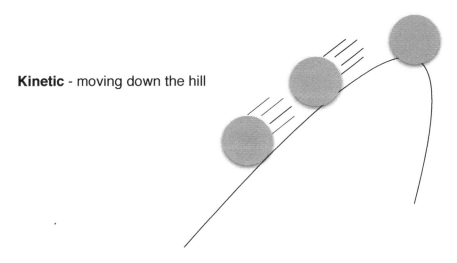

Kinetic - moving down the hill

Also a swing being pulled to the top before it is released has potential energy.

Potential - at the top of the pendulum.

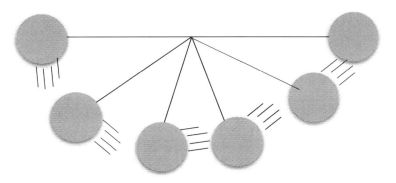

Kinetic - moving through the pendulum

Types of Energy

Type	What it does...	Examples
mechanical	objects in motion	a swing
electrical	moving through the wire	light bulb
chemical	stored in food (fuel)	photosynthesis, lighting a match, rusting
thermal	moving particles	boing water

Heat Transfer

Heat transfer is the exchange of thermal energy between physical systems.

Convection - the transfer of heat by the actual movement of the warmed matter. For example, in a convection oven, air is moved by a fan around the food.

Conduction - the transfer of heat from particle to particle. For example, if a cold spoon is placed in hot soup, the spoon will get hotter until the soup and the spoon become the same temp.

Radiation - the transfer of heat from electromagnetic waves through space. Sunlight is a form of radiation.

Electricity

Electricity can be defined as the flow of an electric charge. The most familiar electricity is the type used in homes and businesses to power lights and appliances. Electrical circuits allow electricity to flow in a loop and power different things.

> **Quick Tip**: When a circuit is open the loop is not closed; therefore, the light will not turn on. Only when the circuit is closed can the electricity travel around the loop fully and light the bulb.

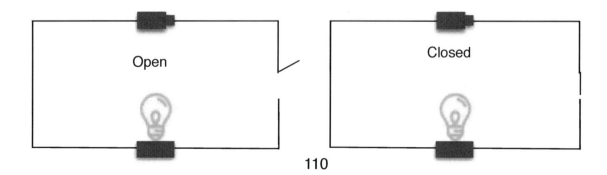

Types of Circuits

Series Circuits - the components are arranged end to end. The electric current flows through the first component, then through the next component and so on, until it reaches the battery again. Below is an example of a series circuit.

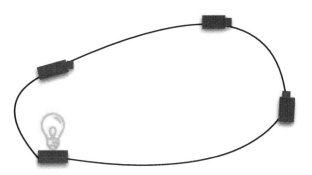

Parallel Circuits - a circuit with branches that allows for multiple applications to happen at once. Below is an example of a parallel circuit.

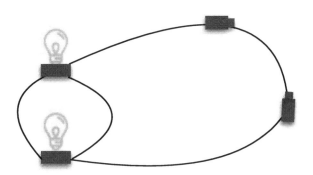

Conductors - good for electricity
- wire
- metal
- water

Insulators - bad for electricity
- rubber
- cloth
- Styrofoam

Forces

A force is any interaction that, when unopposed, will change the motion of an object. Basically, a force can cause an object with mass to change its velocity (which includes to begin moving from a state of rest).

Push

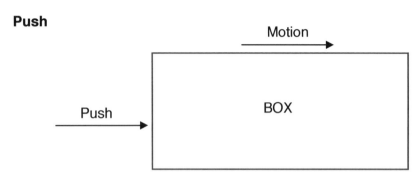

Pull

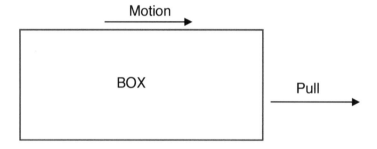

Friction - the force resisting the relative motion of solid surfaces, fluid layers, and material elements sliding against each other.

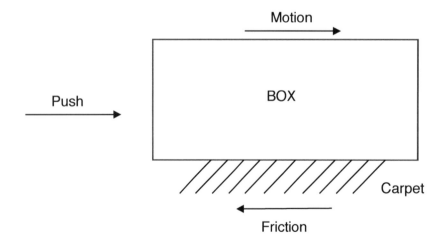

Competency 4 - Knowledge of Earth space

1. Identify characteristics of geologic formations (e.g., volcanoes, canyons, mountains) and the mechanisms by which they are changed(e.g., physical and chemical weathering, erosion, deposition).
2. Identify and distinguish among major groups and properties of rocks and minerals and the processes of their formations.
3. Identify and analyze the characteristics of soil, its components and profile, and the process of soil formation.
4. Identify and analyze processes by which energy from the Sun is transferred (e.g., radiation, conduction, convection) through Earth's systems (e.g., biosphere, hydrosphere, geosphere, atmosphere, cryosphere).
5. Identify and analyze the causes and effects of atmospheric processes and conditions (e.g., water cycle, weather, climate).
6. Identify and analyze various conservation methods and their effectiveness in relation to renewable and nonrenewable natural resources.
7. Analyze the Sun-Earth-Moon system in order to explain repeated patterns such as day and night, phases of the Moon, tides, and seasons.
8. Compare and differentiate the composition and various relationships among the objects of our Solar System (e.g., Sun, planets, moons, asteroids, comets).
9. Identify major events in the history of space exploration and their effects on society.

Geologic Formations & Rocks

Geologic formations are formations made from rocks that exist on the lithosphere. Examples include volcanoes, mountains and canyons.

Mountains are formed as a result of Earth's tectonic plates smashing together.

Volcanos are formed when magma from within the Earth's upper mantle erupts through the surface.

Canyons are formed by weathering and erosion caused by the the movement of rivers. Canyons are also formed by tectonic activity.

Plates Tectonics - the theory that Earth's outer shell is divided into several plates that glide over the mantle or the rocky inner layer above the core. The plates move and separate, causing the Earth to separate and change.

Earthquakes are usually caused when rock underground suddenly breaks along a fault. This sudden release of energy causes the seismic waves that make the ground shake.

- **Divergent** - pulling apart
- **Convergent** - coming together
- **Subduction** - the sideways and downward movement of the edge of a plate into the mantle beneath another plate

Earth's Layers:

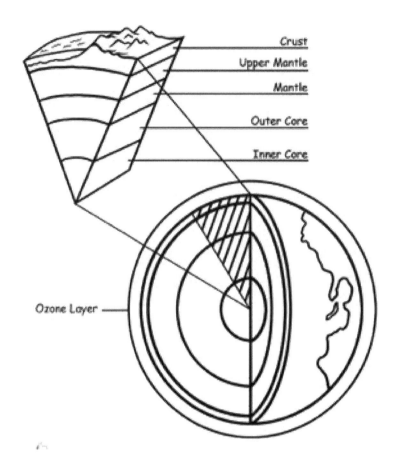

Labels: Crust, Upper Mantle, Mantle, Outer Core, Inner Core, Ozone Layer

Rocks

Type	Igneous	Metamorphic	Sedimentary
Made from...	lava, magma	heat pressure	deposition, cementation
Looks like...	glassy, smooth surface, gas bubble holes, random arrangement of minerals	sparkly crystals, ribbon-like layers	sand grains or visible pebbles. Fossils may also be visible.
Examples	granite, pumice, obsidian	marble, slate, gneiss	conglomerate, sandstone, limestone, shale

Soil is a mixture of minerals, organic matter, gases, liquids, and many organisms that together support life on Earth.

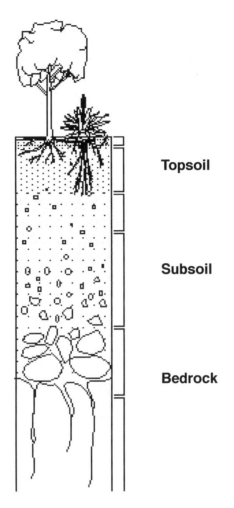

Topsoil

Subsoil

Bedrock

Earth's Systems

Water Cycle

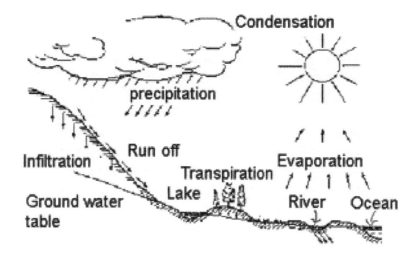

The Earth is made up of different types of spheres.

- **Hydrosphere** - all the water on Earth in liquid form. For example, lakes rivers, oceans are all part of the hydrosphere.
- **Biosphere** - the global sum of all ecosystems.
- **Lithosphere** - the outermost shell of the Earth. The Earth's crust is the lithosphere.
- **Cryosphere** - the masses of frozen water. For example, frozen lakes, rivers, open and glaciers are part of the cryosphere.

Earth, Sun and Moon

Earth is the third planet from the Sun, the densest planet in the Solar System, the largest of the Solar System's four terrestrial planets, and the only astronomical object known to harbor life.

> **Quick Tip:**
> The sun is a star. The reason the sun appears so big is because it is closest to the earth.

The **Sun** is the star at the center of the Solar

> **Quick Tip:**
> When we drive cars, **carbon dioxide** (CO_2) is released into the atmosphere. That CO_2 gets trapped inside the ozone layer and prevents the Sun's rays from escaping. That's why the Earth is heating up.

System. It is the most important source of energy for life on Earth.

The **Moon is** the earth's only natural satellite. The Moon is thought to have formed approximately 4.5 billion years ago, not long after Earth.

A **lunar eclipse** occurs when the Moon passes directly behind the Earth into its umbra (shadow).

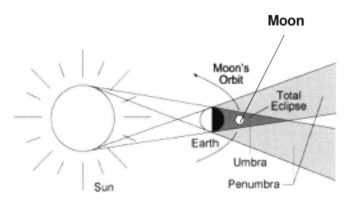

Seasons

We have seasons because of the **Earth's tilt on its axis.** When the Earth is tilted towards the sun, it is warmer (summer). When the earth is tilted away from the sun, it is colder (winter).

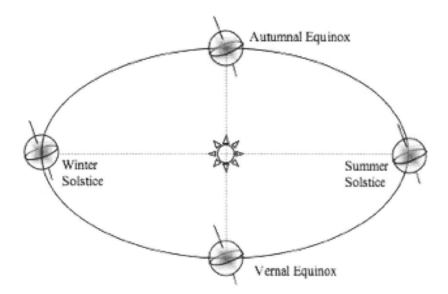

Moon
The Moon affects the tides. In addition, when the Moon is getting bigger, or when its face is more visible, it is waxing. When the Moon is getting smaller or less visible, it is waning.

Phases of the Moon

Celestial Bodies

Comets - a chunk of ice and rock originating outside of the solar system.
Asteroids - a chunk of rock and metal in orbit in between Mars and Jupiter.
Meteorite - a small asteroid.

A bit of history:
The Space Race is a time when the U.S. was competing with Russia to put a man on the moon first. The competition began when the Russians were the first to launch Sputnik, the very first artificial satellite, in 1957. After that, the U.S. committed to getting to the moon before Russia, and called on all scientists, technology specialists, engineers and mathematicians to work towards the common goal. Yes, STEM started back in 1957!

Competency 5 - Knowledge of life science

1. Identify and compare the characteristics of living and nonliving things.
2. Analyze the cell theory as it relates to the functional and structural hierarchy of all living things.
3. Identify and compare the structures and functions of plant and animal cells.
4. Classify living things into major groups (i.e., Linnaean system) and compare according to characteristics (e.g., physical features, behaviors, development).
5. Compare and contrast the structures, functions, and interactions of human and other animal organ systems (e.g., respiration, reproduction, digestion).
6. Distinguish among infectious agents (e.g., viruses, bacteria, fungi, parasites), their transmission, and their effects on the human body.
7. Identify and analyze the processes of heredity and natural selection and the scientific theory of evolution.
8. Analyze the interdependence of living things with each other and with their environment (e.g., food webs, ecosystems, pollution).
9. Identify and analyze plant structures and the processes of photosynthesis, transpiration, and reproduction (i.e., sexual, asexual).
10. Predict the responses of plants to various stimuli (e.g., heat, light, gravity).
11. Identify and compare the life cycles and predictable ways plants and animals change as they grow, develop, and age.

Life

Living things have physical entities and biological processes, such as homeostasis, cell division, cellular respiration and photosynthesis. Nonliving things do not have these process and are classified as *inanimate*.

Cell Theory is made up of three components:
1. All living things are made of cells.
2. The cell is the smallest unit of life.
3. All cells come from preexisting cells.

The organization of life is as follows:

Cells ➤ Tissues ➤ Organs ➤ Organ Systems ➤ Organisms

Plant Cells vs Animal Cells

Plant Cells	Animal Cells
cell wall	plasma membrane
chloroplast	mitochondria
photosynthesis (CO_2 + H_2O + light = Carbohydrates)	cellular respiration (Carbohydrates + O_2 = CO_2 and H_2O

The classification of living things was first done by Carl Linnaeus, as set forth in his *Systema Naturae* (1735). In the taxonomy of Linnaeus there are three kingdoms, divided into classes, which divide into orders, families, genera (singular: genus), and species (singular: species).

- **Domains (ONLY 3)** - Archea, Eubacteria, Eukaryote
- **Kingdom** - Plantae, Animalia, Fungi, Protists, Eubacteria (Monera), Archaebacteria
- **Phylum**
- **Class**
- **Order**
- **Family**
- **Genus**
- **Species - smallest classification**

Energy Pyramid- Here is an example of one type of energy pyramid. Keep in mind that there is an energy pyramid for all ecosystems.

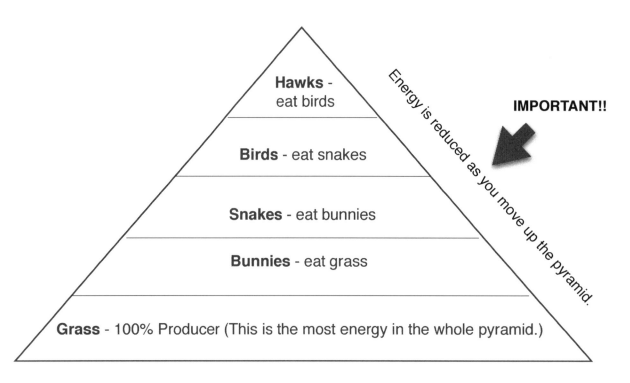

Structures and Functions of Humans an Animals

Circulatory Systems - an organ system that permits blood to circulate and transport nutrients through an organism's body. There are two types of circulatory systems: open and closed.

1. **Open Circulatory System** - a primitive circulatory system where blood doesn't remain enclosed in the tubes or vessels and comes in direct contact with the body cells or tissues.
   - invertebrates
   - mollusks
   - insects
2. **Closed Circulatory System** - a sophisticated and elaborate system as compared to open circulatory system. In closed circulatory system, blood is restricted in the blood vessels during circulation.
   - vertebrates
   - humans
   - snakes
   - cows

Sickness:

Common cold - why is there no antivirus for the common cold?

- The cold can be caused by nearly 250 different viruses. It's just too hard for scientists to make a vaccine that protects you against all of them. Also, from a medical point of view, there's less need to create a vaccine for colds than other illnesses.

Informed Consent - Necessary to perform experiments on human subjects. For example, scientists need informed consent to test new drugs on patients.

Energy Conversion:

1. **Photosynthesis (PLANTS)** is a process used in plants to convert light energy from the Sun into chemical energy that can be later released as fuel in the form of carbohydrates for other organisms.

> **Quick Tip:**
> A plant needs light to survive. In fact, a plant will grow towards the light if it is in a room. It's called **phototropism**. Photo means light. Tropism means growth!

2. **Cellular respiration (ANIMALS)** is a set of metabolic reactions and processes that take place in the cells of animals to convert energy acquired from plants into ATP.

Follow a drop of blood:
1. Blood enters the right atrium from the superior and inferior venae cavae.
2. Then it goes through the tricuspid valve to the right ventricle.
3. From the right ventricle, it goes through the pulmonary semilunar valves the pulmonary trunk
4. From the pulmonary trunk it moves into the right and left pulmonary arteries to the lungs.
5. From the lungs, oxygenated blood is returned to the heart through the pulmonary veins.
6. From the pulmonary veins, blood flows into the left atrium.
7. From the left atrium, blood flows through the bicuspid (mitral) valve int the left ventricle.
8. From the left ventricle, it goes through the aortic semilunar valves into the ascending aorta.
9. Blood is distributed to the rest of the body (systemic circulation) from the aorta.

> **Quick Tip:**
> The pathway of blood in the body goes from right to left. So choose the answer that has the heart traveling right and then left.

Heredity and Genes

Heredity is the passing on of physical or mental characteristics genetically from one generation to another.

Mendel was named the "father of genetics" because of his work with pea plants and heredity. Mendel cross pollinated pea plants and figured out dominate and recessive traits.

Dominance in when the effect of one phenotype of one allele masks the contribution of a second allele at the same locus.The first allele is dominant and the second allele is recessive. For example, in humans, brown eyes is dominant over blue eyes. For a person to display blue eyes, she must have both recessive alleles.

> The only way recessive alleles can show themselves, is if a person inherits all recessive alleles.

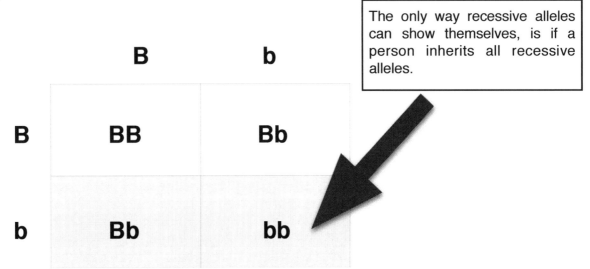

Practice Test - Science

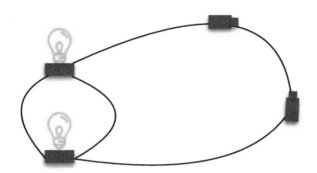

1. The above picture shows what type of circuit?
   A. The batteries are on a series circuit while the light bulbs are on a parallel circuit.
   B. The batteries are on a parallel circuit and the light bulbs are on a parallel circuit.
   C. The batteries are on a series circuit and the lightbulbs are on a series circuit.
   D. The batteries are on a parallel circuit and the light bulbs are onC a parallel.

2. These rocks were originally liquid, below the earth's crust and are formed by lava and magma.
   A. sedimentary
   B. igneous
   C. metamorphic
   D. fossils

3. This type of rock is formed by heat and pressure.
   A. fossil
   B. sedimentary
   C. igneous
   D. metamorphic

4. A river flows through a canyon and picks up a bunch of silt. That sediment and silt runs downstream and deposits where the river ends. When that material gets to the beach, it sits there. Over millions of years, _____ form.
   A. fossils
   B. sedimentary rocks
   C. igneous rocks
   D. metamorphic

5. Mr. Lopez is teaching a unit on seasons. He explains why summer days are longer and winter days are shorter. What should Mr. Lopez emphasize regarding the Earth when explaining this phenomenon?
   A. Earth's revolution around the Sun
   B. Earth's tilt on its axis
   C. Earth's position in the Solar System
   D. Earth's distance away from the Sun

6. The sun appears bigger than other stars because of:
   A. the size of the Sun.
   B. the size of the Solar System.
   C. the distance the Earth is from the Sun.
   D. the distance the sun is from Mars.

7. The _____ affects the ocean tides.
   A. Moon
   B. Sun
   C. stars
   D. Solar System

8. What keeps the earth from falling into the sun?
   A. There is a fairly constant gravitational force between the sun and the earth keeping the earth in its orbit.
   B. Kepler's law and Newtons laws.
   C. The Earth is not moving fast enough to "escape" the Sun's gravity and leave the solar system, but it is going too fast to be pulled into the Sun.
   D. All of the above.

9. The best way for a student to understand the sexual reproductive organs of a flower is to:
   A. read about it in the textbook.
   B. look at a diagram of a flower.
   C. dissect a flower and examine its reproductive organs.
   D. draw a flower and label its reproductive organs.

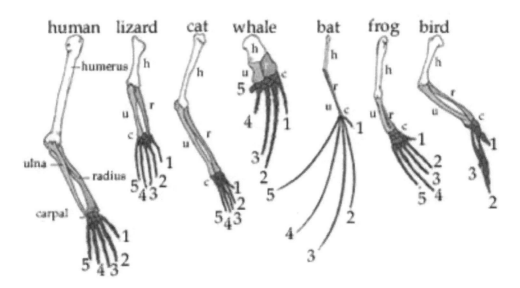

10. The above diagram shows:
    A. natural selection
    B. common ancestry
    C. evolution
    D. classification

11. As random genetic mutations occur within an organism's genetic code, the beneficial mutations are preserved because they aid survival. This is called:

    A. common ancestry.

    B. natural selection.

    C. dominant traits.

    D. recessive traits.

12. Evolution occurs in:

    A. organisms.

    B. kingdoms.

    C. individuals.

    D. populations.

13. The 6 different kingdoms are:

    A. plante, animalia, fungi, protista, eubacteria, archaebacteria.

    B. phylum, animalia, fungi, protista, eubacteria, archaebacteria.

    C. plante, animalia, fungi, protista, eubacteria, prokaryote.

    D. plante, animalia, fungi, protista, eukaryote, archaebacteria.

14. Ms. Smith is teaching her students that cells divide to make other cells. Ms. Smith is teaching:

    A. evolution.

    B. natural selection.

    C. cell theory.

    D. classification.

15. Ms. Rodriguez wants students to understand the diet of an owl. The best way for students to understand this is by:

    A. dissecting an owl pellet (owl poop).

    B. researching owls in an encyclopedia.

    C. reading a chapter on owls in the textbook.

    D. using a Venn diagram to compare and contrast the owl diet with the hawk diet.

16. Mr. Jackson takes his students outside to the sidewalk where a puddle of water has just evaporated. He asks a student to place her hand where the puddle was and the other hand where there was no puddle of water. The sidewalk will feel:

    A. the same temperature for both where the puddle was and where there was no puddle.

    B. cooler where the puddle was than where there was no puddle.

    C. cooler where there was no puddle than where the puddle was.

    D. the temperature cannot be determined through touch. He would need a heat thermometer.

17. The particles in an atom that are negatively charged are:

    A. electrons.

    B. protons.

    C. neutrons.

    D. protons and neutrons together.

18. The gravitational pull of two objects depends on:
    A. the gravity of the two objects.
    B. the mass of the two objects.
    C. the atomic make-up of the two objects.
    D. the electrons in the two objects' atoms.

19. Metals are good _____ in that electric current can flow freely down/through them.
    A. insulators
    B. components
    C. contractors
    D. conductors

20. In a magnet, opposite sides _____ and same sides _____.
    A. attract, attract
    B. repel, attract
    C. attract, repel
    D. repel, repel

21. A tree going through photosynthesis is using what type of energy?
    A. chemical energy
    B. mechanical energy
    C. solar energy
    D. electrical energy

22. _____ are atoms that have lost or gained one or more _____.
    A. compounds, electrons
    B. ions, elections
    C. compounds, protons
    D. ions, protons

23. These are made up of atoms that are held together by chemical bonds.
    A. molecules
    B. electrons
    C. protons
    D. particles

24. _____ happen when warmer, lighter air at the Equator moves toward the cooler air at the poles.
    A. convection currents
    B. conduction currents
    C. atmospheric currents
    D. jet streams

25. _____ are made up of metals and rocky material, while _____ are made up of ice, dust and rocky material.
    A. comets, asteroids
    B. asteroids, comets
    C. meteors, comets
    D. asteroids, meteors

26. This event in history was pivotal in that it galvanized the U.S. space program and started what is known as the Space Race.
    A. building of the Russian Space Station
    B. U.S. astronauts walking on the moon
    C. The Challenger explosion
    D. The launch of Russia's Sputnik

Water Cycle

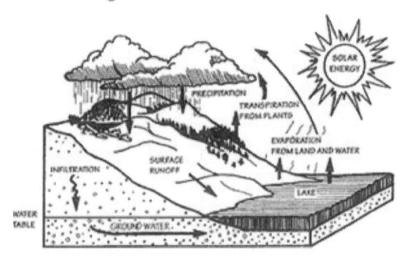

27. The above picture is an example of the:
    A. geosphere.
    B. cryosphere.
    C. biosphere.
    D. hydrosphere.

28. When metal rusts, this is called:
    A. chemical weathering.
    B. erosion.
    C. physical weathering.
    D. deposition.

29. The earth is getting hotter because:
    A. high levels of oxygen trap the Sun's radiation in the atmosphere.
    B. high levels of sodium trap the Sun's radiation in the atmosphere.
    C. high levels of carbon monoxide trap the Sun's radiation in the atmosphere.
    D. high levels of carbon dioxide trap the Sun's radiation in the atmosphere.

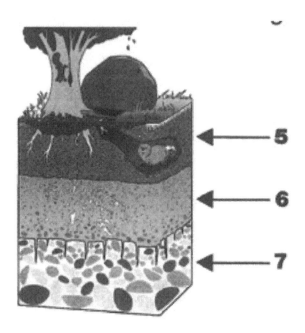

30. In the diagram above, number 6 is:
    A. topsoil
    B. subsoil
    C. bedrock
    D. lava

31. When salt is dissolved in water it disappears. However, you can still taste the salt. This is called:
    A. compound.
    B. solution.
    C. colloid.
    D. suspension.

32. Mr. Jasper wants to show students when oil and water are shaken, no matter how hard, the oil can still be seen as little oil bubbles throughout the mixture. Mr. Jasper is showing the class a:
    A. homogenous mixture.
    B. heterogeneous mixture.
    C. solution.
    D. colloid.

33. Ms. Francis wants to conduct a lab with her students. What is the best way to ensure safety, efficiency and student learning?
    A. Get students into groups to learn on their own.
    B. Predetermine groups, conduct the lab and debrief.
    C. Predetermine groups, assign specific roles for each student, and require a lab journal write-up.
    D. Go over the scientific method to ensure students understand the process of the lab.

34. What would be the best way to demonstrate friction?
    A. Roll a skateboard down the sidewalk and then on the grass to show the difference in speed.
    B. Have students rub their hands together rapidly to observe the heat produced.
    C. Have students rub a balloon on their heads and watch their hair stand up.
    D. Both A and B

35. A rock sitting on top of a hill has what kind of energy?
    A. potential
    B. kinetic
    C. mechanical
    D. chemical

36. When you push a box through the doorway, you are using
    A. chemical energy.
    B. kinetic energy.
    C. mechanical energy.
    D. potential energy.

37. Mr. Lopez wants to conduct a DNA extraction lab but doesn't have the expensive materials necessary to complete the process. What can Mr. Lopez do to maximize the students' learning even though they can't physically do the lab?
    A. Go through a lab simulation with similar items used in a DNA extraction lab.
    B. Have students draw the process on a big sheet of poster paper.
    C. Utilize a web-based virtual lab that can be projected on a screen or SmartBoard in the front of the class.
    D. Have students role play the lab.

38. The best way for a group of students to collect and organize different data points, such as measures of plant growth by date, would be to use a:
    A. spreadsheet.
    B. database.
    C. lab journal.
    D. wiki.

39. If a plant is growing in the corner of the room, the plant will most likely grow towards:
    A. the light.
    B. the window.
    C. the AC.
    D. the students.

40. One of the biggest differences in plant cells and animal cells is:
    A. animal cells have a cell wall and plant cells have a cell membrane.
    B. plant cells have a cell wall and animal cells have a cell membrane.
    C. animal cells have mitochondria and plant cells have chloroplasts.
    D. Both B and C.

41. Punnet squares were first introduced by _____ to determine _____.
    A. Mendel, inheritance
    B. Punnet, genotype
    C. Newton, genotype
    D. Mendel, inheritance

42. This animal has an open circulatory system:
    A. cow
    B. fish
    C. grasshopper
    D. snake

43. The levels of organization, from smallest to largest, within an organism are:
    A. cell, tissues, organ, organ systems, organism.
    B. tissues, organ, organ systems, organism, cells.
    C. organ, tissues, cells, organ systems, organisms.
    D. organisms, organ systems, organs, tissues, cells.

44. Eukaryotic organisms are _____, and prokaryotic organisms are _____.
    A. single cellular, multicellular
    B. multicellular, single cellular
    C. multicellular, multicellular
    D. single cellular, single cellular

45. A science teacher, who works with chemicals in her room, should store the chemical manual:
    A. in the principal's office.
    B. in a locked cabinet in her classroom.
    C. in another teacher's room, where she can access it when she needs to.
    D. in her classroom where it can easily be accessed by anyone who needs it.

46. What would be the best way for a teacher to ensure her monolingual students, who are learning English, understand the complex lesson she will teach on cell division?
    A. Provide monolingual students materials in their native language along with text in English.
    B. Provide monolingual students materials only in English. They need to learn learn English eventually anyway.
    C. Provide monolingual students pictures to go along with the complex English text.
    D. Pair monolingual students with advanced English speaking students for paired reading.

47. In an experiment to see if fertilizer works on a cactus, students have two cacti. Both cacti get the same water and sunlight. Both cacti are in the same place within the room; the temp is the same for both cactus. However, one cactus gets fertilizer, and the other does not. Identify the independent variable and the dependent variable.

    A. The independent variable is the sunlight. The dependent variable is the fertilizer.

    B. The independent variable is the fertilizer. The dependent variable is the growth of the cacti in centimeters.

    C. The independent variable is the cactus that did not get fertilizer. The dependent variable is the sun.

    D. The independent variable is the fertilizer. The dependent variable is the sun.

48. Which would be the best way to activate students' curiosity of the world around them?

    A. Have students go outside and identify as many living and nonliving things as they can.

    B. Have students draw as many living and non-living things as they can.

    C. Have students compete to see how many living and non living things they can identify.

    D. Have students research on the computer living and nonliving things.

49. What would be the best way to demonstrate the difference in growth of the two cacti?

    A. line graph

    B. pie graph

    C. bar graph

    D. splatter plot

50. What would be the best way for a teacher to assess how students apply the scientific method?

    A. Formatively asses students by walking around the lab and watch how students apply the scientific method.

    B. Use a teacher-made multiple choice assessment with scientific method questions.

    C. Administer a state-mandated assessment that assesses the standards for scientific method.

    D. Survey students to identify their understanding of the scientific method.

51. A primary telescope uses a _____ lens.

    A. refractive

    B. reflective

    C. opaque

    D. transitional

52. In a lunar eclipse what is the order of the Earth, Sun, and Moon?

    A. Sun, Earth, Moon

    B. Earth, Moon, Sun

    C. Moon, Earth, Sun

    D. Earth, Sun, Moon

Answers - Science Practice Test

1. A	16. B	31. B	46. A
2. B	17. A	32. B	47. B
3. D	18. B	33. C	48. A
4. B	19. D	34. D	49. C
5. B	20. C	35. A	50. A
6. C	21. A	36. C	51. B
7. A	22. B	37. C	52. A
8. D	23. A	38. A	
9. C	24. A	39. A	
10. B	25. B	40. D	
11. B	26. D	41. B	
12. D	27. D	42. C	
13. A	28. A	43. A	
14. C	29. D	44. B	
15. A	30. B	45. D	

Answer Explanations - Science

1. **A**. A parallel circuit has two or more paths for an electric current to flow through. A series circuit has only one path.
2. **B**. Igneous rocks are formed from magma or lava.
3. **D**. Heat and pressure create metamorphic rocks.
4. **B**. Sedimentation is the process that causes mineral and/or organic particles to settle in place and become sedimentary rocks.
5. **B**. The seasons are caused as the Earth, tilted on its axis, travels around the Sun. Summer happens in the hemisphere tilted towards the Sun, and winter happens in the hemisphere tilted away from the Sun.
6. **C**. The Sun is a star 93 million miles away. However, it appears bigger than other stars because the Earth is closer to the Sun. Other stars are 100,000 times farther away than the Sun.
7. **A**. Tides rise and fall because of the gravitational forces of the moon and sun on the oceans of the earth.
8. **D**. The Earth is not moving fast enough to "escape" the Sun's gravity and float away. The Earth is also going too fast to be pulled into the Sun. Kepler's Second Law of Planetary Motion describes the speed of a planet traveling in an elliptical orbit around the sun. Newton's Law of Gravitation is also applied to planetary functions.
9. **C**. Dissection in science is ideal when it is ethical and appropriate. It is appropriate and ethical for students to dissect a flower to learn about the sexual organs of the plant.
10. **B**. In biology, common ancestry refers to a group of organisms who share a most recent common ancestor. This diagram shows similar hand bones which indicates common ancestry.
11. **B**. Natural selection is the process whereby organisms better adapted to their environment tend to survive and produce more offspring.
12. **D**. Evolution is a change in the gene pool of a population over time.
13. **A**. The six kingdoms are: Plants, Animals, Protists, Fungi, Archaebacteria, Eubacteria. Phylum is a rank above class and below kingdom. Prokaryotes and Eukaryotes are types of cells.
14. **C**. Cell theory has three parts: all living things are made of cells; cells com from pre-existing cells (they divide); and cells are the basic unit of life.
15. **A**. Dissecting owl pellets (owl poop) is the best way to see the diet of an owl. In the pellets students will often find small bones of tiny rodents. Kids love dissecting poop!!
16. **B**. During evaporation liquids cool down. The liquid left behind has less energy than it did before evaporation occurred. Therefore, the temperature of the liquid is lower. Evaporation cools.
17. **A**. Electrons are subatomic particles with a negative charge.
18. **B**. The force of gravity depends directly upon the masses of the two objects.
19. **D**. An electrical conductor is a substance in which electrical charges, usually electrons, move easily from atom to atom with the application of voltage. Metals are good conductors.
20. **C**. A magnet's north pole is attracted to the south pole. Opposites attract and same sides repel.
21. **A**. Plants convert light energy into chemical energy that is used to build molecules of glucose.
22. **B**. An ion is a charged atom or molecule. It is charged because the number of electrons do not equal the number of protons in the atom or molecule. It has lost or gained an electron.

23. **A**. A molecule is the smallest particle in a chemical element or compound that has the chemical properties of that element or compound.
24. **A**. As the cold, heavy air at the poles moves toward the Equator, a constant flow of air convection currents occurs.
25. **B**. Asteroids are made up of metals and rocky material, while comets are made up of ice, dust and rocky material.
26. **D**. The Russian launch of Sputnik began the Dawn of the Space Age. On October 4, 1957, the Soviet Union successfully launched Sputnik and everything about space exploration changed. It launched the U.S. into the Space Race.
27. **D**. Hydro means water. The picture is of the water cycle, therefore it is the hydrosphere.
28. **A**. Chemical weathering is the erosion or disintegration of rocks and metals caused by chemical reactions (chiefly with water and substances dissolved in it) rather than by mechanical processes.
29. **D**. Increased levels of carbon dioxide have caused a gradual increase in the average temperature of the Earth's atmosphere and its oceans.
30. **B**. The top layer of soil is called topsoil. The layer under top soil is sub soil (sub means under.). The rock below the subsoil is bedrock.
31. **B**. A solution is a liquid mixture in which the solute (the salt) is uniformly distributed within the solvent (the water). *Hetero* means different.
32. **B**. A heterogeneous mixture contains components that are not uniform, such as oil and water.
33. **C**. In science instruction, teachers should predetermine groups, organize activities, and be specific on instructions. The more organized and systematic the lesson is, the more effective it will be.
34. **D**. Both choices A and B demonstrate friction; C demonstrates static electricity.
35. **A**. Potential energy is the energy stored in an object as the result of its vertical position or height.
36. **C**. Mechanical energy is the sum of kinetic and potential energy on an object that is used to do work.
37. **C**. Virtual labs are an effective way to provide students with lab experiences. Virtual labs are less expensive and safer than standard labs. If a teacher doesn't have the resources for a complete class lab, a virtual lab is an effective alternative.
38. **A**. A spread sheet is used to store and organize lots of different data (numbers and measurements).
39. **A**. Because plants need light for photosynthesis, plants engage in phototropism, which means they grows towards the light. Photo means light.
40. **D**. Plant cells have cell walls, while animal cells have a plasma membranes. Plant cells have chloroplasts (photosynthesis), while animal cells have mitochondria (cellular respiration).
41. **B**. Punnet squares are named after the person who introduced them, Reginald P. Punnet. The squares are used to determine genotype (expressed traits).
42. **C**. In an open circulatory system, blood and oxygen flow through open spaces within the animal. Invertebrates tend to have open circulatory systems.
43. **A**. The cell is the smallest unit of life, according to Cell Theory. Those cells clump together to make tissues. Tissues make organs. Organs combine with other organs to make organ systems. And organ systems, like the circulatory and respiratory systems, combine to make the organism.
44. **B**. Eukaryotic cells contain membrane-bound organelles, such as the nucleus, while prokaryotic cells do not.
45. **D**. In case of an emergency, the chemical manual should be easily accessible for anyone.

46. **A**. Teachers should provide monolingual students with resources in their native language whenever possible.
47. **B**. The independent variable is the thing changed by the researcher, in this case, the fertilizer. The dependent variable is the observed change, in this case, growth.
48. **A**. Getting students outside and interacting with the real world is an effective way to get students involved in science.
49. **C**. A bar graph can show the growth of more than one variable.
50. **A**. A performance-based, formative assessment, in this case, observing students during a lab, is the best way to assess the skills in applying the scientific method.
51. **B**. A primary telescope uses a mirror in the lens. The mirror *reflects* light.
52. **A**. A lunar eclipse occurs when the Moon passes directly behind the Earth into its umbra (shadow). The order is Sun, Earth, Moon during a lunar eclipse.

Additional Practice - Science

An important skill in slaying the test, is the ability to transfer knowledge from one area to another. That way, no matter how the questions are worded, you have the transfer skills and the flexible thinking to answer accurately. We find that writing your own items for each sub-skill on the test is a great way to sharpen your transfer skills. When you write your own test questions while studying, you're thinking like a test maker and not a test taker!

The following pages provide you an opportunity to write your own test questions for each competency and its sub-skills.

Competency 1 - Knowledge of effective science instruction

sub-skill	test question	answer choices
Analyze and apply developmentally appropriate researched-based strategies for teaching science practices.		
Select and apply safe and effective instructional strategies to utilize manipulatives, models, scientific equipment, real-world examples, and print and digital representations to support and enhance science instruction.		
Identify and analyze strategies for formal and informal learning experiences to provide science curriculum that promotes students' innate curiosity and active inquiry (e.g., hands-on experiences, active engagement in the natural world, student interaction).		
Select and analyze collaborative strategies to help students explain concepts, to introduce and clarify formal science terms, and to identify misconceptions.		
Identify and apply appropriate reading strategies, mathematical practices, and science-content materials to enhance science instruction for learners at all levels.		
Apply differentiated strategies in science instruction and assessments based on student needs.		

Identify and apply ways to organize and manage a classroom for safe, effective science teaching that reflect state safety procedures and restrictions (e.g., procedures, equipment, disposal of chemicals, classroom layout, use of living organisms).		
Select and apply appropriate technology, science tools and measurement units for students' use in data collection and the pursuit of science.		
Select and analyze developmentally appropriate diagnostic, formative and summative assessments to evaluate prior knowledge, guide instruction, and evaluate student achievement.		
Choose scientifically and professionally responsible content and activities that are socially and culturally sensitive.		

Competency 2 - Knowledge of effective science instruction

sub-skill	test question	answer choices
Analyze the dynamic nature of science models, laws, mechanisms, and theories that explain natural phenomena (e.g., durability, tentativeness, replication, reliance on evidence).		
Identify and apply science and engineering practices through integrated process skills (e.g., observing, classifying, predicting, hypothesizing, designing and carrying out investigations, developing and using models, constructing and communicating explanations).		
Differentiate between the characteristics of experiments (e.g., multiple trials, control groups, variables) and other types of scientific investigations (e.g., observations, surveys).		
Identify and analyze attitudes and dispositions underlying scientific thinking (e.g., curiosity, openness to new ideas, appropriate skepticism, cooperation).		
Identify and select appropriate tools, including digital technologies, and units of measurement for various science tasks.		
Evaluate and interpret pictorial representations, charts, tables, and graphs of authentic data from scientific investigations to make predictions, construct explanations, and support conclusions.		

Identify and analyze ways in which science is an interdisciplinary process and interconnected to STEM disciplines (i.e., science, technology, engineering, mathematics).		
Analyze the interactions of science and technology with society including cultural, ethical, economic, political, and global factors.		

Competency 3 - Knowledge of physical sciences

sub-skill	test question	answer choices
Identify and differentiate among the physical properties of matter (e.g., mass, volume, texture, hardness, freezing point).		
Identify and differentiate between physical and chemical changes (e.g., tearing, burning, rusting).		
Compare the properties of matter during phase changes through the addition and/or removal of energy (e.g., boiling, condensation, evaporation).		
Differentiate between the properties of homogeneous mixtures (i.e., solutions) and heterogeneous mixtures.		
Identify examples of and relationships among atoms, elements, molecules, and compounds.		
Identify and compare potential and kinetic energy.		
Differentiate among forms of energy, transformations of energy, and their real-world applications (e.g., chemical, electrical, mechanical, heat, light, sound).		
Distinguish among temperature, heat, and forms of heat transfer (e.g., conduction, convection, radiation).		
Analyze the functionality of an electrical circuit based on its conductors, insulators, and components.		
Identify and apply the characteristics of contact forces (e.g., push, pull, friction), at-a-distance forces (e.g., magnetic, gravitational, electrostatic), and their effects on matter (e.g., motion, speed).		

Competency 4 - Knowledge of Earth space

sub-skill	test question	answer choices
Identify characteristics of geologic formations (e.g., volcanoes, canyons, mountains) and the mechanisms by which they are changed(e.g., physical and chemical weathering, erosion, deposition).		
Identify and distinguish among major groups and properties of rocks and minerals and the processes of their formations.		
Identify and analyze the characteristics of soil, its components and profile, and the process of soil formation.		
Identify and analyze processes by which energy from the Sun is transferred (e.g., radiation, conduction, convection) through Earth's systems (e.g., biosphere, hydrosphere, geosphere, atmosphere, cryosphere).		
Identify and analyze the causes and effects of atmospheric processes and conditions (e.g., water cycle, weather, climate).		
Identify and analyze various conservation methods and their effectiveness in relation to renewable and nonrenewable natural resources.		
Analyze the Sun-Earth-Moon system in order to explain repeated patterns such as day and night, phases of the Moon, tides, and seasons.		
Compare and differentiate the composition and various relationships among the objects of our Solar System (e.g., Sun, planets, moons, asteroids, comets).		
Identify major events in the history of space exploration and their effects on society		

Competency 5 - Knowledge of life science

sub-skill	test question	answer choices
Identify and compare the characteristics of living and nonliving things.		
Analyze the cell theory as it relates to the functional and structural hierarchy of all living things.		
Identify and compare the structures and functions of plant and animal cells.		
Classify living things into major groups (i.e., Linnaean system) and compare according to characteristics (e.g., physical features, behaviors, development).		
Compare and contrast the structures, functions, and interactions of human and other animal organ systems (e.g., respiration, reproduction, digestion).		
Distinguish among infectious agents (e.g., viruses, bacteria, fungi, parasites), their transmission, and their effects on the human body.		
Identify and analyze the processes of heredity and natural selection and the scientific theory of evolution.		
Analyze the interdependence of living things with each other and with their environment (e.g., food webs, ecosystems, pollution).		
Identify and analyze plant structures and the processes of photosynthesis, transpiration, and reproduction (i.e., sexual, asexual).		
Predict the responses of plants to various stimuli (e.g., heat, light, gravity).		
Identify and compare the life cycles and predictable ways plants and animals change as they grow, develop, and age.		

This page is intentionally left blank.

IV. Mathematics

This chapter provides an overview of the competencies for the mathematics section of Elementary ED (K-6) Subject Area Exam. This section has explanations regarding all the competencies tested on the exam as well as in depth analysis of the types of questions students will encounter when taking this test.

The competencies addressed in this chapter are from the Florida Teacher Certification Examination Test Information Guide.

You can access that using this link:
http://www.fl.nesinc.com/PDFs/ElemEd_K-6_TIG_4thEd_DOE040115.pdf

Competency 1 - Knowledge of student thinking and instructional practices

1. Analyze and apply appropriate mathematical concepts, procedures, and professional vocabulary (e.g., subitize, transitivity, iteration, tiling) to evaluate student solutions.
2. Analyze and discriminate among various problem structures with unknowns in all positions in order to develop student understanding of operations (e.g., put-together/take-apart, arrays/area).
3. Analyze and evaluate the validity of a student's mathematical model or argument (e.g., inventive strategies, standard algorithms) used for problem solving.
4. Interpret individual student mathematics assessment data (e.g., diagnostic, formative, progress monitoring) to guide instructional decisions and differentiate instruction.
5. Select and analyze structured experiences for small and large groups of students according to the cognitive complexity of the task.
6. Analyze learning progressions to show how students' mathematical knowledge, skills, and understanding develop over time.
7. Distinguish among the components of math fluency (i.e., accuracy, automaticity, rate, flexibility).

Analyze and apply appropriate mathematical concepts

Subitize - knowing the number by looking at a representation of the number. For example, when a person sees 6 dots on a die, he or she knows immediately that it is 6.

Transitivity - a > b
b > c
a > c

Iteration - repeating the same steps over and over again. Anything that is sequential in operation is iteration.

- Ex: using a non-standard unit of measurement, like a paperclip, one after another to measure the length of a desk.
- Ex: following the steps for the standard algorithm in addition.

Tiling - used to represent the abstract as concrete. For example, a teacher can use tiles to represent negative numbers. Tilting can also be used to represent an array for multiplication.

3 x 4

> **Quick Tip:**
>
> The diagram to the left shows an **array**. **Arrays** are useful representations of multiplication concepts and geometric concepts like area. This **array** has 3 rows and 4 columns. It can also be described as a 3 by 4 **array**.

Analyze and discriminate among various problem structures

Elementary math has changed. While the processes are the same, the terminology is different. It it important to understand the math language used on the test. See the table below.

Common addition and subtraction scenarios:

	RESULT UNKNOWN	CHANGE UNKNOWN	START UNKNOWN
ADD TO	Two bunnies sat on the grass. Three more bunnies hopped there. How many bunnies are on the grass now? $2 + 3 = ?$	Two bunnies were sitting on the grass. Some more bunnies hopped there. Then there were five bunnies. How many bunnies hopped over to the first two? $2 + ? = 5$	Some bunnies were sitting on the grass. Three more bunnies hopped there. Then there were five bunnies. How many bunnies were on the grass before? $? + 3 = 5$
TAKE FROM	Five apples were on the table. I ate two apples. How many apples are on the table now? $5-2 = ?$	Five apples were on the table. I ate some apples. Then there were three apples. How many apples did I eat? $5 - ? = 3$	Some apples were on the table. I ate two apples. Then there were three apples. How many apples were on the table before? $? -2 = 3$
	TOTAL UNKNOWN	ADDEND UNKNOWN	BOTH ADDENDS UNKNOWN2
PUT TOGETHER/ TAKE APART	Three red apples and two green apples are on the table. How many apples are on the table? $3 + 2 = ?$	Five apples are on the table. Three are red and the rest are green. How many apples are green? $3 + ? = 5, 5-3 = ?$	Grandma has five flowers. How many can she put in the red vase and how many in her blue vase? $5 = 0 + 5, 5 + 0$ $5 = 1 +4, 5 = 4 +1$ $5 = 2 + 3, 5 = 3 + 2$
COMPARE	DIFFERENCE UKNOWN How many more? Lucy has two apples. Julie has five apples. How many more apples does Julie have than Lucy?("How many fewer?" version): Lucy has two apples. Julie has five apples. How many fewer apples does Lucy have then Julie? $2 + ? = 5, 5 - 2 = ?$	BIGGER UNKNOWN What changes? Julie has three more apples than Lucy. Lucy has two apples. How many apples does Julie have? (Version with "fewer"): Lucy has 3 fewer apples than Julie. Lucy has two apples. How many apples does Julie have? $2 + 3 = ?, 3 + 2 = ?$	SMALLER UNKNOWN Julie has three more apples than Lucy. Julie has five apples. How many apples does Lucy have? (Version with "fewer"): Lucy has 3 fewer apples than Julie. Julie has five apples. How many apples does Lucy have? $5 – 3 = ?, ? + 3 = 5$

(National Governors Association Center for Best Practices, Council of Chief State School Officers, 2016)

Common multiplication and division situations.

	UNKNOWN PRODUCT	GROUP SIZE UNKNOWN ("HOW MANY IN EACH GROUP?" DIVISION)	NUMBER OF GROUPS UNKNOWN ("HOW MANY GROUPS?" DIVISION)
	$3 \times 6 = ?$	$3 \times ? = 18$, and $18 \div 3 = ?$	$? \times 6 = 18$, and $18 \div 6 = ?$
EQUAL GROUPS	There are 3 bags with 6 plums in each bag. How many plums are there in all? Measurement example: You need 3 lengths of string, each 6 inches long. How much string will you need altogether?	If 18 plums are shared equally into 3 bags, then how many plums will be in each bag? Measurement example: You have 18 inches of string, which you will cut into 3 equal pieces. How long will each piece of string be?	If 18 plums are to be packed 6 to a bag, then how many bags are needed? Measurement example: You have 18 inches of string, which you will cut into pieces that are 6 inches long. How many pieces of string will you have?
ARRAYS, AREA	There are 3 rows of apples with 6 apples in each row. How many apples are there? Area example: What is the area of a 3 cm by 6 cm rectangle?	If 18 apples are arranged into 3 equal rows, how many apples will be in each row? Area example: A rectangle has area 18 square centimeters. If one side is 3 cm long, how long is a side next to it?	If 18 apples are arranged into equal rows of 6 apples, how many rows will there be? Area example:A rectangle has area 18 square centimeters. If one side is 6 cm long, how long is a side next to it?
COMPARE	A blue hat costs $6. A red hat costs 3 times as much as the blue hat. How much does the red hat cost? Measurement example: A rubber band is 6 cm long. How long will the rubber band be when it is stretched to be 3 times as long?	A red hat costs $18 and that is 3 times as much as a blue hat costs. How much does a blue hat cost? Measurement example: A rubber band is stretched to be 18 cm long and that is 3 times as long as it was at first. How long was the rubber band at first?	A red hat costs $18 and a blue hat costs $6. How many times as much does the red hat cost as the blue hat? Measurement example: A rubber band was 6 cm long at first. Now it is stretched to be 18 cm long. How many times as long is the rubber band now as it was at first?
GENERAL	$a \times b = ?$	$a \times ? = p$ and $p \div a = ?$	$? \times b = p$, and $p \div b = ?$

(National Governors Association Center for Best Practices, Council of Chief State School Officers, 2016)

MULTIPLICATIVE COMPARISON	The giraffe is 18 feet tall. She is 3 times as tall as the kangaroo. How tall is the kangaroo?	The giraffe in the zoo is 3 times as tall as the kangaroo. The kangaroo is 6 feet tall. How tall is the giraffe?	The giraffe is 18 feet tall. The kangaroo is 6 feet tall. The giraffe is how many times taller than the kangaroo?
MULTIPLICATIVE COMPARISON	The giraffe is 18 feet tall. The kangaroo is 1/3 as tall as the giraffe. How tall is the kangaroo?	The kangaroo is 6 feet tall. She is 1/3 as tall as the giraffe. How tall is the giraffe?	The giraffe is 18 feet tall. The kangaroo is 6 feet tall. What fraction of the height of the giraffe is the height of the kangaroo?

Common Core Leadership in Mathematics Project, University of Wisconsin-Milwaukee, 2011-2012 School Year

Analyze and evaluate the validity of a student's mathematical model or argument

Inventive Strategies are methods in which students invent ways to solve complex problems. They involve using reason and understanding to get to the end result. Here are some examples of inventive strategies students use:

- **Partitioning** - taking large numbers and splitting them into small, manageable units.

- **Compensation** - borrowing pieces of one number to compensate for another to make it easier to solve.

Partitioning	Compensation
467 - 122 =	46 + 38 =
400 - 100 = 300	Take **4** from the **38** and give it to the 46.
60 - 20 = 40	
7 - 2 = 5	50 + 34 =
345	**84**

Standard Algorithm is a specific method of computation which is conventionally taught for solving particular mathematical problem using standard notation in:

- exchanging
- regrouping
- long division
- long multiplication
- average
- area
- volume

Interpret individual student mathematics assessment data

All assessments used in a classroom should be aligned to the state standards. Teachers planning math instruction, developing lessons, and assessing students should always start with the state standards first.

Diagnostic - an assessment that measures students' skills at the beginning of a unit or lesson. Think of this as a baseline.

Formative - ongoing observations, assessments that happen during instruction to gauge student learning and to make instructional adjustments.

Summative - used at the end of learning to measure mastery of the standards.

Progress Monitoring - continuously and systematically looking at student progress and making instructional decisions accordingly.

Scenario:

Mr. Rodriguez wants to see where his students are before he begins a unit. He knows that students must have fluency in their addition and subtraction facts before they can be successful on the unit. He decides to give the students a timed diagnostic test that will assess the students' adding and subtraction skills. He will use the data from the diagnostic test to plan and make further curriculum decisions regarding the addition facts.

Analyze structured experiences for small and large groups of students according to the cognitive complexity of the task

Tiered Ability Grouping:

- **Compacting** - groups of students who can skip steps and move quickly because they have advanced math fluency.
- **Interest grouping** - groups of students based on student interest.
- **Flexible grouping** - groups change from day to day and even within a class period.

Progression of Math Knowledge Over Time and Math Fluency

Students evolve as they learn math. Understanding math is just like understanding anything: you start with the concrete and move toward the abstract.

Think CRA!

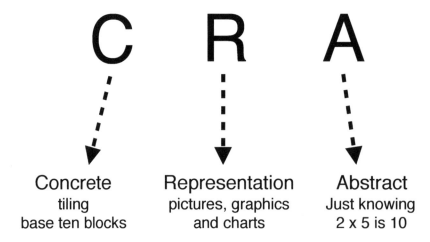

C	R	A
Concrete	**Representation**	**Abstract**
tiling	pictures, graphics	Just knowing
base ten blocks	and charts	2 x 5 is 10

Math Fluency

Rate - How fast can the student solve problems?
Accuracy - How many problems did the student get correct?
Automaticity - Does the student have quick automatic facts memorized? Can the student quickly recite these facts (i.e. multiplication facts)?
Flexibility - Can the student solve the problem in different ways?

Competency 2 - Knowledge of operations, algebraic thinking, counting and number in base ten

1. Interpret and extend multiple representations of patterns and functional relationships by using tables, graphs, equations, expressions, and verbal descriptions.
2. Select the representation of an algebraic expression, equation, or inequality that models a real-world situation.
3. Analyze and apply the properties of equality and operations in the context of interpreting solutions.
4. Determine whether two algebraic expressions are equivalent by applying properties of operations or equality.
5. Evaluate expressions with parentheses, brackets, and braces.
6. Analyze and apply strategies (e.g., models, estimation, reasonableness) to solve multistep word problems.
7. Apply number theory concepts (e.g., primes, composites, multiples, factors, parity, rules of divisibility).
8. Identify strategies (e.g., compensation, combining tens and ones) based on place value to perform multi digit arithmetic.

Interpret and extend multiple representations of patterns

Properties of Operations

Associative property of addition	$(a + b) + c = a + (b+c)$
Commutative property of addition	$a + b = b + a$
Additive identity property of 0	$a + 0 = 0 + a = a$
Existence of additive inverses	For every a there exists -a so that $a + (-a) = (-a) + a = 0$
Associative property of multiplication	$(a \times b) \times c = a \times (b \times c)$
Commutative property of multplication	$a \times b = b \times a$
Multiplicative identity property of 1	$a \times 1 = 1 \times a = a$
Existence of multiplicative inverses	For every $a = 0$ there exists 1/a so that $a \times 1/a = 1/a \times a = 1$
Distributive propery of multiplication over additions	$a \times (b + c) = a \times b + a \times c$

(National Governors Association Center for Best Practices, Council of Chief State School Officers, 2016)

> **Quick Tip:**
>
> **4(x + 2)**
>
> The correct way of saying this is **4 times the quantity x+2.**

Properties of Equality

Reflexive property of equality	$a = a$.
Symmetric property of equality	If $a = b$, then $b = a$.
Transitive property of equality	If $a = b$ and $b = c$, then $a = c$.
Addition property of equality	If $a = b$, then $a + c = b + c$.
Subtraction property of equality	If $a = b$ then $a - c = b - c$.
Multiplication property of equality	If $a = b$, then $a \times c = b \times c$.
Division property of equality	If $a = b$ and $c \neq 0$, then $a \div c = b \div c$.
Substitution property of equality	If $a = b$, then b may be substituted for a in any expression containing a.

(National Governors Association Center for Best Practices, Council of Chief State School Officers, 2016)

Properties of Inequalities
Exactly one of the following is true: $a < b$, $a = b$, $a > b$.
If $a > b$ and $b > c$ then $a > c$.
If $a > b$, $b < a$.
If $a > b$, then $-a < -b$.
If $a > b$, then $a \pm c > b \pm c$.
If $a > b$ and $c > 0$, then $a \times c > b \times c$.
If $a > b$ and $c < 0$, then $a \times c < b \times c$.
If $a > b$ and $c > 0$, then $a \div c > b \div c$.
If $a > b$ and $c < 0$, then $a \div c < b \div c$.

(National Governors Association Center for Best Practices, Council of Chief State School Officers, 2016)

Sample Question:
If $ab = c$ then,

a. $b = \dfrac{c}{a}$

b. $b = \dfrac{a}{c}$

c. $b = \dfrac{a}{b}$

d. $b = \dfrac{b}{c}$

> **HINT:**
> Since all the answer choices are in $b =$, get b alone. To get the **b** alone next to the equal sign, divide both sides by **a**. **The answer is A.**

Greatest Common Factor vs Least Common Multiple

Greatest Common Factor (GCF)
The greatest common factor, or GCF, is the greatest factor that divides two numbers. To find the GCF of two numbers:

- list the prime factors of each number.
- multiply those factors both numbers have in common.
- if there are no common prime factors, the GCF is 1.

For **20** and **50:**

20's prime factors are 2, 5.
50's prime factors are 2, 5.

2 x 5 = 10
Therefore, 10 is the GCF of 20 and 50.

Remember! 1 is NOT a prime number.

Least Common Multiple (LCM)
The least common multiple is the smallest positive number that is a multiple of two or more numbers. Example: the Least Common Multiple of 3 and 5 is 15. Because 15 is a multiple of 3 and 5, it is the smaller of the two numbers and therefore the least common multiple.

*Look at the Factor Tree below. You can see that the smallest factors of 24 is 3, and 2.

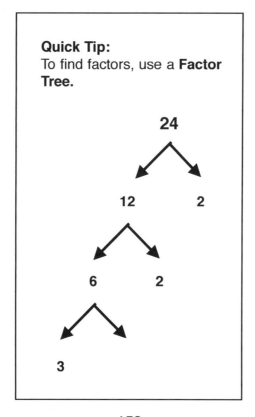

Quick Tip:
To find factors, use a **Factor Tree.**

Competency 3 - Knowledge of fractions, ratios, and integers

1. Compare fractions, integers, and integers with integer exponents and place them on a number line.
2. Convert among standard measurement units within and between measurement systems (e.g., metric, U.S. customary) in the context of multistep, real-world problems.
3. Solve problems involving addition, subtraction, multiplication, and division of fractions, including mixing whole numbers and fractions, decimals and percents by using visual models and equations to represent the problems and their solutions.
4. Select the representation (e.g., linear, area, set model) that best represents the problem and solution, given a word problem or equation involving fractions.
5. Solve real-world problems involving ratios and proportions.

Fractions

To add or subtract fractions, **find the common denominator,** then add or subtract.
To multiply fractions, **multiply straight across.** No common denominator is needed.
To divide fractions, **multiply by the reciprocal.**

$$\frac{5}{8} \div \frac{3}{4} = \frac{5}{8} \text{ X } \frac{4}{3} = \frac{20}{24} = \frac{5}{6}$$

To turn improper fractions into mixed numbers, divide the numerator by the denominator and put the remainder over the denominator:

$$42 \div 5 = 8 \text{ remainder } 2$$

$$\frac{42}{5} = 8 \frac{2}{5}$$

To turn mixed numbers into improper fractions, multiple the denominator by the whole number and add the numerator.

$$5 \text{ x } 8 = 40$$
$$40 + 2 = 42$$

$$8 \frac{2}{5} = \frac{42}{5}$$

Proportions and Ratios

Yolanda wants to build a ramp. For every 5 inches high the ramp is, the base must be 8 inches long. She decides to only make the ramp 10 inches high. How many inches long should the ramp be?

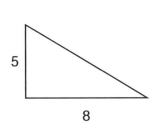 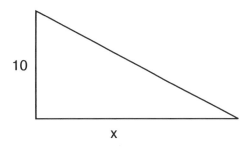

Set this up like a proportion. Make the two ramps equal and solve.

$$\frac{5}{8} = \frac{10}{X}$$

Cross multiply.

$$\frac{5}{8} \quad \diagtimes \quad \frac{10}{X}$$

$$5x = 80$$

x = 16

The length of the base should be 16 in.

Select the representation that best represents the problem and solution, given a word problem or equation involving fractions

Sam had 12 pieces of gum. He was told by his teacher to divide it equally among him and his 3 friends. Below is how he divided the pieces of gum. What mistake did he make in this situation?

He grouped incorrectly. There should be 4 groups of three. He was told to divvy the gum among him and his 3 friends. That's 4 people, not 3.

Be able to identify errors in regrouping.

$$\begin{array}{r} 201 \\ -130 \\ \hline 171 \end{array}$$

In the above problem, the student did not regroup after subtracting in the tens column.

Understand where numbers fall on a number line.

Look at the following numbers. In what order do they fall on the number line?

1, -10, .33, 5/8, -1.3, 3/2, 0, -1

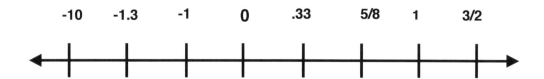

Competency 4 - Knowledge of measurement, data, and statistics

1. Calculate and interpret statistics of variability (e.g., range, mean absolute deviation) and central tendency (e.g., mean, median).
2. Analyze and interpret data through the use of frequency tables and graphs.
3. Select appropriate measurement units to solve problems involving estimates and measurements.
4. Evaluate the choice of measures of center and variability, with respect to the shape of the data distribution and the context in which the data were gathered.
5. Solve problems involving distance, time, liquid volume, mass, and money, which may include units expressed as fractions or decimals.

Solve problems involving distance, time, liquid volume, mass, and money.

If you are trying to figure out how many miles per hour you went in a day, use the formula m/h.

1. You are traveling to Tallahassee, and you know that you've been traveling for 5 hours. You have been going an average speed of 75 miles per hour. How many miles have you gone?

   Set it up: Speed = Distance/Time

$$\frac{m}{5} = 75$$

   Use algebra to solve by multiplying both sides by 5. **You have traveled 375 miles.**

2. You are taking a road trip and drive 500 miles in 8 hours the first day. On the second day you drive 300 miles in 6 hours. What is the difference in speed between the two days of travel?

$$\frac{500}{8} - \frac{300}{6}$$

$$62.5 - 50 = \textbf{12.5}$$

   There is a difference of **12.5 mph between the two days.**

VOLUME

In some of the problems on the test, you will be required to convert volume measures.

You have 3876 mL of water during your soccer practice. Your friend comes over and guzzles down 1.5 L of your water. How many mL do you have left?

First we have to convert the 1.5L to mL. There are 1000 mL in a L. Therefore, your friend guzzled down 1500 mL of your 3876mL.

Then, subtract 1500 from 3876. That equals 2376.

You have 2376 mL left.

How many L do you have left?
Convert 2376 to L by moving the decimal 3 spaces (1000). 2376 mL is 2.376 L.

You have 2.376 L left

MONEY

Jan gets paid $18.50 dollars per hour. For any work done over 40 hours she gets time and a half. What is her total paycheck if she works 48 hours?

       i)   reg pay - 18.50 x 40 = 740
       ii) over time pay -18.50 x 1.5 = 27.75 x 8 (hours of overtime) = 222
       iii) 740 + 222 = $962.00 total paycheck

Competency 5 - Knowledge of geometric concepts

1. Apply geometric properties and relationships to solve problems involving perimeter, area, surface area, and volume.
2. Identify and locate ordered pairs in all four quadrants of a rectangular coordinate system.
3. Identify and analyze properties of three-dimensional shapes using formal mathematical terms such as volume, faces, edges, and vertices.
4. Classify two-dimensional figures in a hierarchy based on mathematical properties.

Apply geometric properties and relationships to solve perimeter, area, surface area, and volume

You build a pool with a length of 12 and a width of 8. You need to add a walkway around the pool. However, you only have 190 sq. ft. to work with. How much space do you have left for the walkway?

    i.   12 ft x 8 ft = 96 sq. ft.
    ii. 190 sq. ft. is the total space you have.
    iii. 190 - 96 = 94.
    iv. You have 94 sq. ft. left to build the walkway.

AREA

You need 2 pieces of cardboard for a project. The first is a right triangle with measurements 3, 4, 5. The other is a right triangle twice as large. What is the total area of the two pieces of cardboard? What is the difference in the area of the two pieces of cardboard?

First figure out the measurement of the 3, 4, 5 triangle, which is 6, 8, 10.

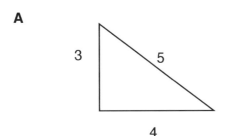

Then figure out the area of both triangles by using the formula 1/2(b x h).

A. 4 x 3 = 12 times 1/2 is 6
B. 8 x 6 = 48 times 1/2 is 24

Answer:
- The total area of both triangles is **30**.
- The difference in the area of the two triangles is **18**.

Identifying Geometric Shapes

right triangle

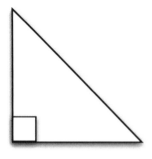

isosceles right triangle

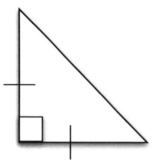

obtuse triangle

acute triangle

Practice Test

1. A plot of land has perimeter dimensions of 165' x 100'. How much of the land is left after a house 1/5 the size of the property is placed on the land?
   a. 13200
   b. 16500
   c. 12000
   d. 15300

2. What is 4^3 ?
   a. 16
   b. 12
   c. 64
   d. 72

3. What is 6^{-2} ?

   a. $\dfrac{1}{6}$

   b. $\dfrac{1}{12}$

   c. $\dfrac{1}{36}$

   d. $\dfrac{1}{48}$

4. What is -5^2 ?
   a. -25
   b. 25
   c. 10
   d. -10

5. 3/8 + 2/3?
   a. 25/24
   b. 3/7
   c. 7/9
   d. 1/4

6. The two triangles are similar. What is X?

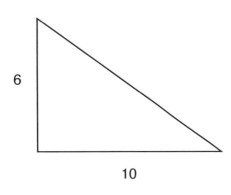 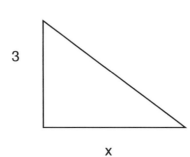

    a. x = 6
    b. x = 10
    c. x = 4
    d. x = 5

7. Julie buys 6 apples at $0.50 each, 4 rolls of paper towels at $1.50 each and 2 six-packs of soda at $3 .50 each. She gives the teller a $20 bill. What change must the teller give back to Julie?
    a. $4.00
    b. $4.50
    c. $5.00
    d. $5.50

8. Mary makes costume bracelets and sells them at the market. It costs Mary $0.30 per bracelet for beads and $1.50 per bracelet for chain. Mary also pays a one-time booth rental fee of $60. If Mary sells 200 bracelets at $4.00 each, what is her profit?
    a. $480
    b. $350
    c. $380
    d. $120

9. 4 students are working on completing a book together for their English class. Julie has completed 1/6 of the book. Jose has completed 1/3 of the book. Amelia has completed 1/4 of the book. How much left is there for Roberto to complete so the book is finished?
    a. 3/4
    b. 1/4
    c. 2/3
    d. 1/3

10. A farmer sells bushels of pears for $20 per bushel plus a one-time $2.00 surcharge to each customer. If t = total money paid by one customer and b = the number of bushels sold to that customer, what equation in terms of *t* and *b* would apply?
    a. 20b + 2.00 = t
    b. 2b + 20 = t
    c. 20 + t = b
    d. 20b + t = 2

11. A student is solving the following equation:

$$4(x + 3) - 5(x + 3) \div 3 = 0$$

At what step did the student make her initial mistake?

Step 1: 4x + 12 − 5x − 15 ÷ 3 = 0
Step 2: −1x − 3 ÷ 3 = 0
Step 3: −1x − 1 = 0
Step 4: x = −1

    a. Step 1
    b. Step 2
    c. Step 3
    d. Step 4

12. A bike originally priced at $350 is put on clearance for $150. What is the percentage discount?
    a. 47%
    b. 57%
    c. 37%
    d. 46%

13. Harry puts $1000 into his savings account. The account is yielding 6% annually. If he does not touch the money nor put any more into the account, how much money will Harry have in the account at the end of 3 years?
    a. $1191
    b. $1180
    c. $1020
    d. $1600

14. What is an equation for 5 less than twice a number?
    a. 5 − 2n
    b. 2n − 5
    c. 5n − 2
    d. 2 − 5n

15. Which figure is showing the most surface area?

A. 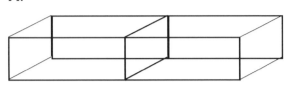　　　　　　　　　　　　**B.**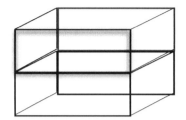

    a. A
    b. B
    c. A & B
    d. Cannot be determined.

16. A teacher is rolling a die on a desk and asking her student to say the number on the die by simply looking at it. When a student does this, the student is:
    a. tiling.
    b. estimating.
    c. subitizing.
    d. transitioning.

17. A student is solving the problem 536 + 43 + 27. The student decides to break the problem down like this:

$$500 + 40$$
$$30 + 20$$
$$6 + 3 + 7$$

The student is using what method to solve the problem?
    a. subitizing
    b. estimating
    c. iteration
    d. partitioning

18. What is the correct order of a student's thought process in geometry?
    a. abstract, concrete, representation
    b. representation, abstract, concrete
    c. concrete, abstract, representation
    d. concrete, representation, abstract

19. $(a + b) + c = a + (b+c)$ is an example of:
    a. associative property.
    b. additive property.
    c. commutative property.
    d. distributive.

20. What is the greatest common factor of 32 and 24?
    a. 3
    b. 4
    c. 6
    d. 8

21. Lucy has two apples. Julie has five apples. How many more apples does Julie have than Lucy? This is an example of:
    a. compare bigger unknown.
    b. compare difference unknown.
    c. put-together total unknown.
    d. put-together additive unknown.

22. If a = b, then b = a is an example of:
    a. reflexive property.
    b. transitive property.
    c. communicative property.
    d. symmetric property.

23. A student draws three circles and crosses two out during a subtraction lesson. She is using what type of learning method?
    a. concrete
    b. representation
    c. abstract
    d. flexibility

24. Find the next term in the pattern 7, 14, 21, 28…
    a. 32
    b. 35
    c. 36
    d. 42

For questions 25-28 use the information below.

Students in the class received the following scores on a quiz worth 10 points.

7, 5, 5, 6, 7,10, 9, 9, 6, 8, 8, 8, 8, 4, 2

25. What is the mean score for the class data set?
    a. 5
    b. 6
    c. 7
    d. 8

26. What is the median score for the class data set?
    a. 5
    b. 6
    c. 7
    d. 8

27. What is the mode for class data set?
    a. 5
    b. 6
    c. 7
    d. 8

28. What is the range of the class data set?
    a. 5
    b. 6
    c. 7
    d. 8

29. What is the value of x in 5x + 13 = 23?
    a. 2
    b. 4
    c. 5
    d. 10

30. The expression $f^3 \cdot f^9$ is equal to
    a. f^{12}
    b. f^{27}
    c. 27f
    d. 9f

31. Which of the following expression matches the following narrative?

3 more than 4 times a number

    a. 3(4 + n)
    b. 3 + 4n
    c. 3n + 4n
    d. n(3 + 4)

32. Where would 1/5 go on the following number line?

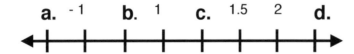

33. Jose, Roberto, Alyssa and Roger are all comparing distances from their houses to school. From school Jose's house is $2\frac{2}{5}$ miles away; Roberto's house is $2\frac{5}{8}$ miles away; Alyssa's house is $2\frac{1}{4}$ away and Roger's house is $2\frac{3}{10}$. Order the students from longest to shortest distance.

    a. Jose, Roger, Alyssa, Roberto
    b. Alyssa, Roger, Jose, Roberto
    c. Roger, Alyssa, Roberto, Jose
    d. Roberto, Jose, Roger, Alyssa

34. Choose the appropriate line graph for the following table.

Growth	Time
0	2
2	4
4	6
6	8

a

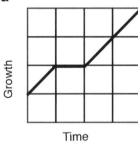

b

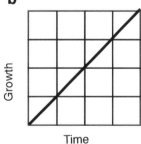

c

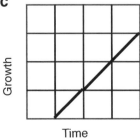

d

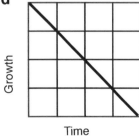

35. The number .67 is equal to
     a. 7/6
     b. 67%
     c. 6.7%
     d. 6/7

36. A teacher is giving an untimed test and is allowing students to solve problems in a multitude of ways. She is looking for:
     a. fluency and rate.
     b. accuracy and rate.
     c. accuracy and flexibility.
     d. flexibility and fluency.

37. The teacher is giving a test that she will use to find students' weaknesses to focus her instruction. She is using a:
     a. formative assessment .
     b. summative assessment.
     c. norm-referenced assessment.
     d. state test assessment.

38. A flagpole casts a shadow that is 12 feet long. A child who is 4 feet tall casts a shadow that is 6 feet long. How tall is the flagpole?
     a. 14 ft.
     b. 12 ft.
     c. 10 ft.
     d. 8 ft.

39. What is $\dfrac{5}{8} + \dfrac{3}{4}$?

    a. $1\dfrac{3}{14}$

    b. $1\dfrac{3}{8}$

    c. $1\dfrac{4}{7}$

    d. $1\dfrac{1}{4}$

40. A restaurant sells popcorn and peanuts. Popcorn is $2.00 a bag and peanuts are $2.50 a bag. How much will the customer spend to buy **a** boxes of popcorn and **b** boxes of peanuts?
    a.   ab(2 + 2.5)
    b.   2a + 2.5b
    c.   2a − 2.5b
    d.   2.5a + 2b

41. Which of the following pairs of factors does NOT have a greatest common factor equal to 8?
    a.   48, 120
    b.   56, 72
    c.   24, 40
    d.   16, 32

42. Solve 4x + 24 = 36

    a.   x = 2
    b.   x = 4
    c.   x = 3
    d.   x = 6

43. If a = b and b = c then:
    a. a = c
    b. ab = c
    c. ac = b
    d. cb = a

44. April has 32 long-sleeved and short-sleeved shirts in her closet. 21 of the shirts are long-sleeved. What percentage of her shirts are short-sleeved?
    a. 66%
    b. 34%
    c. 54%
    d. 24%

45. The coordinates of a line on a graph are (4, 8). If the line is running horizontally, what is another possible set of coordinates?
    a. (8,4)
    b. (6,-5)
    c. (-4, 8)
    d. (-8,4)

46. The coordinates of a line on a graph are (6, 7). If the line is running vertically, what is another possible set of coordinates?
    a. (7,6)
    b. (-7, 6)
    c. (6,-7)
    d. (-6,-7)

47. Which one of the following is the sum of the prime factors of 140?
    a. 12
    b. 14
    c. 16
    d. 22

48. Find the area of the trapezoid.

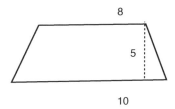

a. 80
b. 45
c. 60
d. 40

49. Which of the following is an appropriate first step in learning the concepts of finding the area of a rectangle?
    a. Use tiles to form arrays and count the squares to figure out the area.
    b. Draw pictures of rectangles and count the perimeter of the rectangle.
    c. Use a geometric formula to solve the problem quickly.
    d. Use cubes to discuss the surface area of a prism.

50. Which of the following would be most effective in assessing students' understanding of the steps in the division process?
    a. a timed multiple choice test on division.
    b. an untimed test where students are required to show their work.
    c. an open book test.
    d. a state assessment focusing on the new math standards.

51. Mary sells handmade earrings at the local street market. She made 3 times as much today as she did yesterday. She made $21 today. What type of problem is this?
    a. comparison division
    b. comparison multiplication
    c. put together
    d. take apart

52. It's 5° below zero in Springfield, MA. By noon the temperature dropped 3 more degrees. What is the temperature at noon?

    a. 8°

    b. 2°

    c. -8°

    d. -3°

53. Solve $1\frac{3}{4} \div \frac{2}{3}$

    a. $2\frac{5}{6}$

    b. $2\frac{1}{2}$

    c. $2\frac{3}{5}$

    d. $2\frac{5}{8}$

54. Solve

$$\frac{x - 7}{6} - \frac{2x + 4}{2} = -4$$

    a. $x = -2$

    b. $x = 2$

    c. $x = -1$

    d. $x = 1$

55. Simplify: $4(x + 3) - 2(x + 6)$

    a. $2x + 24$

    b. $2x$

    c. $2x + 12$

    d. $4x$

56. The teacher is showing students how to divide 66 inches of fabric into 6 - 11in parts. The teacher is using:
    a. array strategy.
    b. base ten strategy.
    c. equal parts strategy.
    d. tiling strategy.

57.

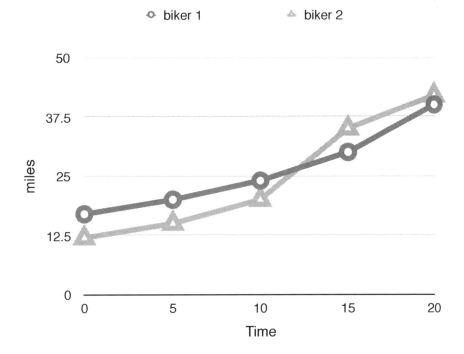

When did biker 2 pass biker one?
    a. 10 min
    b. 12 min
    c. 14 min
    d. 15 min

58. The average arm span of an elementary school student is 1m. Teachers want to show students how far a 1/2 of a kilometer is. How many students should they bring outside to demonstrate a 1/2 of a kilometer?
    a. 1200
    b. 1000
    c. 500
    d. 250

59. A biologist is evaluating the population of salmon in a lake. Initially she catches 200 salmon and tags all of them. A month later she catches 80 and 25 are tagged. She can estimate the population of salmon in the lake is:

    a. 80.

    b. 200.

    c. 640.

    d. 20,000.

60. Which of the following demonstrates the distributive property?

    a. $x(y+z) = xy + xz$

    b. $x(y+z) = xy + z$

    c. $x(y+z) = x(z+y)$

    d. $x(y+z) = zy + x$

Answers - Math Practice Test

1. A	16. C	31. B	46. C
2. C	17. D	32. B	47. B
3. C	18. D	33. D	48. B
4. B	19. A	34. C	49. A
5. A	20. D	35. B	50. B
6. D	21. B	36. C	51. B
7. A	22. A	37. A	52. C
8. C	23. B	38. D	53. D
9. B	24. B	39. B	54. D
10. A	25. C	40. B	55. B
11. B	26. C	41. A	56. C
12. B	27. D	42. C	57. B
13. A	28. D	43. A	58. C
14. B	29. A	44. B	59. C
15. A	30. A	45. C	60. A

Answer Explanations - Math

1. **A.** Find the area of the plot of land (165 x 100 = 16500). Then multiple the area by 1/5 or .20. The result is 3300. Subtract 3300 from 16500. The result is 13,200.
2. **C.** 4 x 4 = 16. 16 x 4 = 64.
3. **C.** Whenever a number is to a negative exponent, the result is 1 over the number (result).
4. **B.** -5 x -5 = 25. A negative times a negative is a positive.
5. **A.** Find the common denominator, then add. It cannot be reduced.
6. **D.** Set the triangles proportional. 6/10 = 3/5
7. **A.** 6 x .50 = $3.00; 4 x 1.50 = $6.00; 2 x 3.50 = $7.00; $3.00 + $6.00 + $7.00 = $16.00. $20.00 − $16.00 = $4.00
8. **C.** It costs Mary $1.80 per bracelet. If she sells them for $4.00 each, she makes $2.20 on each bracelet. She sold 200 of them. 200 x $2.20 = $440.00. However, she has to pay the booth rental for $60.00. $440.00 − $60.00 = $380.00 profit.
9. **B.** Add 1/6, 1/4 and 1/3 by finding a common denominator (24). That gives you 18/24. Reduce it to 3/4. If 3/4 of the book is completed, Roberto has 1/4 left to complete.
10. **A.** 20 dollars per bushel means 20b. The surcharge is just 2.00 because it is a one time charge. If t = the total, the equation is 20t + 2.00 = t.
11. **B.** The first step is correct - the student distributed through the parentheses first. However, in the second step the student added/subtracted when she should have divided first (15 ÷ 3).
12. **B.** $350 − $150 = $200. 200 ÷ 350 = .571428. Or 57%. You can also do this very quickly by thinking $175 is half of $350. Therefore, the bike is more than 50% off. The only answer that is more than 50% is B.
13. **A.** If the account yields 6% annually, the first year the account total $1060. The second year the account earns $63.60 because 6% times 1060 is $63.60. So, the total in the account for the second year is $1123.60. The third year the account earns $67.42 because 6% times $1123.60 is $67.42. The total amount in the account on the third year is $1191.
14. **B.** See below

Phrase	Expression
five less than twice a number	2n - 5
the product of a number and 6	6n
seven divided by twice a number	$7 \div 2n$ or $\dfrac{7}{2n}$
three times a number decreased by 11	3n - 11

15. **A.** In figure a, the smallest sides of the figure are covered. In figure B, the bigger sides of the figure are covered. Therefore, figure A is showing more surface area than figure B.
16. **C.** Subitizing is knowing the number by looking at a representation of the number. Rolling a die and having students quickly identify numbers on the die is a subitizing strategy.
17. **D.** Partitioning is working out problems that involve large numbers by splitting them into smaller units. They are easier to work with this way.
18. **D.** Remember, think *CRA* (concrete, representation, abstract).

19. **A**. See page 151.
20. **D**. The factors for 32 are 2, 4, 8, and 16. The factors for 24 are 2, 3, 4, 6, 8, and 12. The largest number they have in common is 8.
21. **B**. See page 147.
22. **A**. See page 152.
23. **B**. Representation is drawing figures to represent numbers. It is the second stage of math fluency (CRA).
24. **B**. The pattern goes as follows: 7 x 1 = 7; 7 x 2 = 14; 7 x 3 = 21; 7 x 4 = 28; 7 x 5 = 35.
25. **C**. The mean is the average (add all the numbers and divide by how many numbers there are). All the numbers added up is 102. Divide that by the amount of numbers, and you get 6.8 or 7.
26. **C**. Put all the numbers in order to find the median: 2, 4, 5, 5, 6, 6, 7, 7, 8, 8, 8, 8, 9, 9, 10. Since there are 15 numbers, the mean is easy to find. It is the middle number: 7.
27. **D**. The mode is the number that appears the most in the set. 8 appears more often than any other number. The mode is 8.
28. **D**. The range is the largest number minus the smallest number. 10 - 2 = 8.
29. **A**. To solve 5x + 13 = 23, use basic algebra. Subtract 13 from both sides, which gives you 5x = 10. Divide both sides by 5 which gives you x = 2.
30. **A**. Add exponents when you are multiplying.
31. **B**. Break it down: 3 more is + 3. 4 times a number is 4n. Therefore 3 + 4n is the equation.
32. **B**. Make 1/5 into a decimal by dividing 1 by 5 and you get .20. Or you can say that 1/5 is bigger than -1 and less than 1.
33. **D**. Make this problem easy on yourself; only look at the fractions. All the kids are 2 miles away from school. Find a common denominator which is 40. Jose is 16/40, Roberto is 25/40, Alyssa is 10/40, and Roger is 12/40. The order from longest distance to shortest distance is Roberto, Jose, Roger and Alyssa.
34. **C**. The key here is to know that the growth starts at zero, but the time starts at two. Therefore, the graph that starts at 0, 2 is the correct graph.
35. **B**. To find the percent of a decimal, move the decimal point 2 places to the right. .67 as a fraction is 67/100.
36. **C**. If it is an untimed test, the teacher is more concerned with accuracy than she is with rate. She is looking for flexibility when asking students to solve a problem multiple ways.
37. **A**. Remember, formative assessments *inform* instruction.
38. **D**. This is a proportion. Set them equal to each other. x/12 = 4/6. Cross multiply. 6x = 48. x = 8

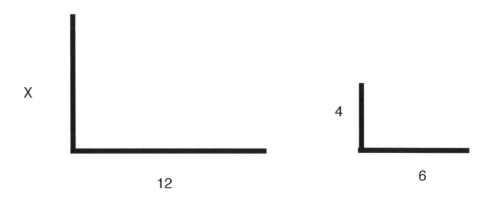

39. **B**. Get a common denominator, which is 8. 5/8 + 6/8 = 11/8. Turn it into a mixed number by dividing 11 by 8. That gives you 1 and 3/8.
40. **B**. Popcorn = a and peanuts = b. Therefore 2a + 2.5b.
41. **A**. The greatest common factor (GCF) of 48 and 120 is 24.
42. **C**. Solve 4x + 24 = 36 by using basic algebra. To get the x alone, subtract 24 from both sides: 4x = 12. Then divide both sides by 4. x = 3.
43. **A**. All the factors are equal to each other; therefore, a = c.
44. **B**. If 21 out of 32 are long sleeve, that means that more than half are long sleeve. That means less than half are short sleeve. That eliminates b and c right away. To find the percentage divide the difference of 32 - 21 = 11. 11 ÷ 32 = 34%.
45. **C**. If the line runs horizontal, the y coordinate stays the same. Therefore, any answer should have 8 as the y coordinate.

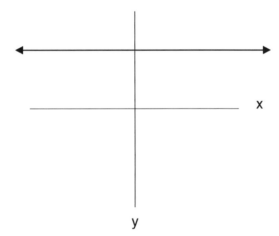

46. **C**. In a vertical line, the x stays the same. Therefore, any answer should have the x coordinate as 6.

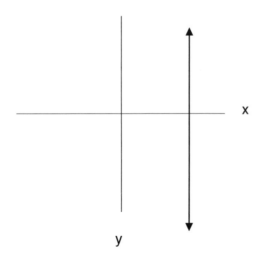

47. **B**. All of the prime factors of 140 are 2, 7, and 5. Remember, 1 is NOT a prime number.
48. **B**. The formula for the area of a trapezoid is (1/2) a + b x (h). 8 + 10 = 18.
    18 x 5 = 90. 90 ÷ 2 is 45.
49. **A**. The key word here is *first*. If a student is in her first step in learning area, she should be using tiles to represent the area in a concrete way. Tiles are for concrete learners, and concrete is the first stage in math fluency.
50. **B**. Assessing understanding requires an untimed test where students show their thought process by showing their work on paper.
51. **B**. See page 148.
52. **C**. 5 below zero is -5. If the temp drops and additional 3 degrees, it is -5 + -3 = 18.
53. **D**. Turn 1 3/4 into the fraction 7/4. Then to divide fractions, you multiply by the reciprocal. It would be 7/4 x 3/2 = 21/8. Then turn 21/8 into a mixed number 2 5/8.
54. **D**. The first thing you have to do with this problem is get a common denominator.

Think of $\dfrac{x - 7}{6}$ $\dfrac{2x + 4}{2}$ as fractions. Get a common denominator. 6 is a common denominator. Multiply both the top and bottom of the second fraction by 3.

That gives you $\dfrac{x - 7}{6} - \dfrac{6x + 12}{6} = -4$

Then simplify the top of the 2 equations. $\dfrac{-5x - 19}{6} = -4$

The use algebra to solve for x. Multiply both sides by 6.

$-5x - 19 = -24$

$-5x = -5$

$x = 1$

55. **B**. To simplify 4 (x + 3) - 2(x + 6), first distribute the 4 and the 2. That gives you:
    4x + 12 − 2x −12. Then combine like terms. 4x − 2x = 2x, and 12 −12 = 0. which gives you 2x.
56. **C**. The fabric is divided into 6 parts of 11. They are equal (66 ÷ 6 = 11). Equal parts strategy is the best choice.
57. **B**. Biker A remains in the lead until roughly half way between the 10th and 15th min. Therefore 12 min is your best choice. 14 min is too close to 15 min. 12 min is the most accurate choice.
58. **C**. A km is 1000m. If a student's arm span is 1m, you would need 1000 kids to show a km. However, you only want a 1/2 of a km, which is 500m. Therefore, you'll need 500 students.

59. **C**. Set this up as a proportion and solve. She tagged all of them the first time and out of 80, 25 were tagged.

$$\frac{200}{x} = \frac{80}{25}$$

Cross multiply. 5000 = 80x. Then solve for x.
x = 640

60. **A**. To solve x (y + z), you must distribute the x, which gives you xy + xz. The distributive property is shown.

Additional Practice - Math

An important skill in slaying the test, is the ability to transfer knowledge from one area to another. That way, no matter how the questions are worded, you have the transfer skills and the flexible thinking to answer accurately. We find that writing your own items for each sub-skill on the test is a great way to sharpen your transfer skills. When you write your own test questions while studying, you're thinking like a test maker and not a test taker!

The following pages provide you an opportunity to write your own test questions for each competency and its sub-skills.

Competency 1: Knowledge of student thinking and instructional practices

sub-skill	test question	answer choices
Analyze and apply appropriate mathematical concepts, procedures, and professional vocabulary (e.g., subitize, transitivity, iteration, tiling) to evaluate student solutions.		
Analyze and discriminate among various problem structures with unknowns in all positions in order to develop student understanding of operations (e.g., put-together/take-apart, arrays/area).		
Analyze and evaluate the validity of a student's mathematical model or argument (e.g., inventive strategies, standard algorithms) used for problem solving.		
Interpret individual student mathematics assessment data (e.g., diagnostic, formative, progress monitoring) to guide instructional decisions and differentiate instruction.		
Select and analyze structured experiences for small and large groups of students according to the cognitive complexity of the task.		
Analyze learning progressions to show how students' mathematical knowledge, skills, and understanding develop over time.		
Distinguish among the components of math fluency (i.e., accuracy, automaticity, rate, flexibility).		

Competency 2: Knowledge of operations, algebraic thinking, counting and number in base ten

sub-skill	test question	answer choices
Interpret and extend multiple representations of patterns and functional relationships by using tables, graphs, equations, expressions, and verbal descriptions.		
Select the representation of an algebraic expression, equation, or inequality that models a real-world situation.		
Analyze and apply the properties of equality and operations in the context of interpreting solutions.		
Determine whether two algebraic expressions are equivalent by applying properties of operations or equality.		
Evaluate expressions with parentheses, brackets, and braces.		
Analyze and apply strategies (e.g., models, estimation, reasonableness) to solve multistep word problems.		
Apply number theory concepts (e.g., primes, composites, multiples, factors, parity, rules of divisibility).		
Identify strategies (e.g., compensation, combining tens and ones) based on place value to perform multi digit arithmetic.		

Competency 3: Knowledge of operations, algebraic thinking, counting and number in base ten

sub-skill	test question	answer choices
Compare fractions, integers, and integers with integer exponents and place them on a number line.		
Convert among standard measurement units within and between measurement systems (e.g., metric, U.S. customary) in the context of multistep, real-world problems.		
Solve problems involving addition, subtraction, multiplication, and division of fractions, including mixing whole numbers and fractions, decimals and percents by using visual models and equations to represent the problems and their solutions.		
Select the representation (e.g., linear, area, set model) that best represents the problem and solution, given a word problem or equation involving fractions.		
Solve real-world problems involving ratios and proportions.		

Competency 4: Knowledge of measurement, data, and statistics

sub-skill	test question	answer choices
Calculate and interpret statistics of variability (e.g., range, mean absolute deviation) and central tendency (e.g., mean, median).		
Analyze and interpret data through the use of frequency tables and graphs.		
Select appropriate measurement units to solve problems involving estimates and measurements.		
Evaluate the choice of measures of center and variability, with respect to the shape of the data distribution and the context in which the data were gathered.		
Solve problems involving distance, time, liquid volume, mass, and money, which may include units expressed as fractions or decimals.		

Competency 5: Knowledge of geometric concepts

sub-skill	test question	answer choices
Apply geometric properties and relationships to solve problems involving perimeter, area, surface area, and volume.		
Identify and locate ordered pairs in all four quadrants of a rectangular coordinate system.		
Identify and analyze properties of three-dimensional shapes using formal mathematical terms such as volume, faces, edges, and vertices.		
Classify two-dimensional figures in a hierarchy based on mathematical properties.		

58441867R00104

Made in the USA
Lexington, KY
11 December 2016